How to Use SPSS®

A Step-by-Step Guide to Analysis and Interpretation

Brian C. Cronk
Missouri Western State College

 Pyrczak Publishing

P.O. Box 39731 • Los Angeles, CA 90039

Notice

SPSS is a registered trademark of SPSS, Inc. Screen images © by SPSS, Inc. and Microsoft Corporation. Used with permission.

This book is not approved or sponsored by SPSS.

Consulting Editor: Jose L. Galvan.

Cover design by Robert Kibler and Larry Nichols.

Editorial assistance provided by Elaine Fuess, Cheryl Alcorn, Brenda Koplin, Ken Ornburn, Ron Matossian, and Randall R. Bruce.

Printed in the United States of America.
10 9 8 7 6 5 4   DOC   04 03 02 01

ISBN 1-884585-15-9

Table of Contents

Introduction

The SPSS statistical package is designed to perform a wide range of statistical procedures. Like any other powerful computer program, there are certain conventions and techniques that must be mastered in order to use the program efficiently and to obtain correct answers consistently. By providing detailed step-by-step guidance illustrated with worked-out examples, this book will help you achieve such mastery.

In addition to showing you how to enter data and obtain results, this book shows you how to select appropriate statistics and state the results in a form that is suitable for use in a research report in the social or behavioral sciences. For example, the section on the independent t test shows how to state (i.e., phrase) the results of both a significant and an insignificant test.

Audience

This book assumes only a basic understanding of statistics. Thus, it is ideal as a supplement to a traditional introductory statistics textbook. It can also be used as a statistics refresher manual in a research methods course. Finally, students can use it as a desk reference guide in a variety of workplace settings after they graduate from college.

SPSS is an incredibly powerful program, and this text does not attempt to be a comprehensive user's manual. Instead, it targets the procedures normally covered in introductory courses in statistics and research methods.

Organization

The book is organized into eight chapters. The first two chapters deal with the basic mechanics of using the SPSS program. Each of the remaining chapters focuses on a particular class of statistics.

Each chapter contains several short sections. For the most part, these sections are self-contained. However, it is expected that students will master the SPSS basics in Chapters 1 and 2 before attempting to learn the skills in the rest of the book. Except for the skills in the first two chapters, the book can be used in a nonlinear manner. Thus, an instructor can assign the first two chapters early in a course, and then assign other sections in whatever order is appropriate.

Appendix A contains a "decision tree" that helps in the selection of appropriate inferential statistics for various research designs. Appendix B contains data sets that are needed for the Practice Exercises that are interspersed throughout this book. The glossary in Appendix C provides definitions of most of the statistical terms used in this book. Because it is assumed that it is being used in conjunction with a main statistics textbook, the glossary definitions are brief and designed to serve only as reminders. Finally, Appendix D provides the sample data files that are used throughout this book.

SPSS Versions

There are numerous variations and versions of the SPSS statistical package. This guide was written for use with the 8.0 version of SPSS for Windows. It can work easily with earlier versions, especially Versions 7.0 and 7.5. However, there are substantial differences in how the output appears between Version 6.1 and later versions. These differences are noted in this book.

The menu bars shown in the illustrations are ones that appear when the Base, Professional, and Advanced modules (the most common modules) of the program have been installed. If your menu bars look different or if you cannot locate a menu item for a command presented in this book, it may be that your institution supports different modules. For instance, some colleges use only the Base module, but the Reliability procedure is available only with the Professional module and the repeated measures ANOVA procedure is available only with the Advanced module. Check with your instructor for additional guidance.

Some institutions purchase site licenses from SPSS to make the software available free of charge to their faculty and, sometimes, their students. If your institution has not purchased a site license, you should still be able to purchase the student version of the software in your campus bookstore at a discounted price for the educational community. Either of these will be a fully functional version of the software intended for your personal use.

Conventions

The following conventions have been used throughout this book.
- Items presented in **bold** are defined or explained in the Glossary in Appendix C.
- Items in *italics* are either buttons or menus from the SPSS program or statistical symbols.
- Items in ALL CAPITAL LETTERS are either acronyms or the names of variables in the SPSS data file.

Practice Exercises

Practice exercises are included for each skill presented. In addition, the skills acquired in this text can be used in doing the practice exercises in other statistics texts or workbooks. One text that would work well in this capacity is *Real Data: A Statistics Workbook.*[1]

Acknowledgments

This book is dedicated to the students in my Behavioral Statistics and Measurements, Research Methods, and Intermediate Statistics courses. While teaching those courses, I became aware of the need for an SPSS manual that did more than simply tell students how to start the program and enter data. I am deeply indebted to Wendy Schweigert at Bradley University, who first showed me the power, simplicity, and usefulness of statistics. This book was field tested in Sally Radmacher's Behavioral Statistics and Measurements course at Missouri Western State College and Wendy Schweigert's course at Bradley University. Jose L. Galvan of California State University, Los Angeles, provided support and helpful suggestions throughout the process. Of course, this text would not have been possible without the support of my wife and family.

---

[1] Holcomb, Z. (1997). *Real Data: A Statistics Workbook.* Los Angeles: Pyrczak Publishing.

Chapter 1

Getting Started

Section 1.1 Starting SPSS

Starting SPSS will differ slightly depending on the exact configuration of the machine on which it is installed. On most Windows 95 and Windows 98 computers, you can start SPSS by first clicking on *Start*, then clicking on *Programs*, then on *SPSS*. On many installations, there will be an *SPSS* icon on the desktop that you can double-click to start the program.

When SPSS is started, you may be presented with the dialog box to the left, depending on the options your system administrator selected for your version of the program. If you have the box, click *Type in data* and *OK*, which will present a blank **data window**.[1]

If you were not presented with the dialog box to the left, SPSS should open automatically with a blank data window.

The data window and the **output window** provide the basic interface for SPSS. A blank data window is shown below.

Section 1.2 Entering Data

One of the keys to success with SPSS is knowing how it stores and uses your data. To illustrate the basics of data entry with SPSS, we will use example 1.2.1.

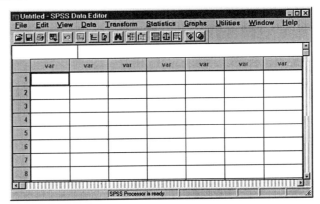

Example 1.2.1

A survey was given to several students in four different classes (Tues/Thurs mornings, Tues/Thurs afternoons, Mon/Wed/Fri mornings, Mon/Wed/Fri afternoons). The students were asked whether or not they were "morning people" and whether or not they worked. This survey also asked their final grade in the class (out of 100). The response sheets from two students are presented as follows:

---

[1] Items that can be looked up in the glossary are presented in **bold**.

Response Sheet 1

ID:	4593		
Day of class:	____ MWF		X TR
Class time:	____ Morning		X Afternoon
Are you a morning person?	____ Yes		X No
Final grade in class:	85%		
Do you work outside of school?	____ Full-time		____ Part-time
	X No		

Response Sheet 2

ID:	1901		
Day of class:	X MWF		____ TR
Class time:	X Morning		____ Afternoon
Are you a morning person?	X Yes		____ No
Final grade in class:	83%		
Do you work outside of school?	____ Full-time		X Part-time
	____ No		

Our goal is to enter the data from the two students into SPSS for use in future analyses. The first step is to determine the variables that need to be entered. Any information that can vary among participants is a variable that needs to be considered. Example 1.2.2 lists the variables we will use.

Example 1.2.2

ID#
Day of class
Time of class
Morning person
Final grade
Whether or not the student works outside of school

In the SPSS data window, columns represent variables and rows represent subjects. Therefore, we will be creating a data file with six columns (variables) and two rows (students/participants).

Section 1.3   Defining Variables

Before we can enter any data, we must first enter into SPSS some basic information about each variable. For instance, each variable must first be given a name that:
- begins with a letter;
- does not contain a space; and
- is eight characters or fewer in length.

Thus, the variable name "Q7" would be acceptable, while the variable name "7Q" would not be. Similarly, the variable name "PRE_TEST" is acceptable, but the variable

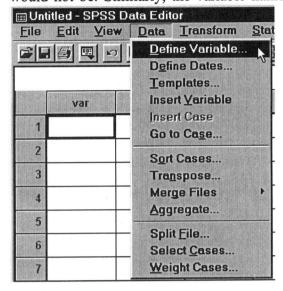

name "PRE TEST" is not. Capitalization does not matter, but variable names are capitalized in this text to make it clear when we are referring to a variable name.

To define a variable, click on *Data* then click on *Define Variable*. This will bring up the Define Variable dialog box shown below. Enter the variable name in the blank near the top ("id" in the example).

From the Define Variable dialog box, SPSS allows you to enter variable labels by clicking on the *Labels* button. Variable labels allow you to associate a description with each variable. These descriptions can describe the variables themselves or the values of the variables. For most procedures, SPSS requires numerical values. Thus, for data such as the day of the class (e.g., Mon/Wed/Fri and Tues/Thurs) we need to first code the values as numbers. For example, we can assign the number 1 to Mon/Wed/Fri and the number 2 to Tues/Thurs. To help us keep track of the numbers we have assigned to the values, we can click on the *Value Label* command.

When you enter a value label, you must click *Add* after each entry. That will move the associated value and label into the bottom section of the window. When all labels have been added, click on *Continue* to return to the Define Variable window.

New with version 8.0 is the ability to indicate the measurement scale on which the variable is measured. You can select Nominal, Ordinal, or Scale. In SPSS, a scale variable is an interval or ratio-scaled variable. You need to select the appropriate measurement scale in the *Measurement* section of the define variable dialog box. Note that this feature applies only to some chart functions.

In addition to naming and labeling the variable, you have the option of defining the variable type. To do so, simply click on the *Type* button (see dialog box to the left). This will bring up the Define Variable Type dialog box shown below. Using this dialog box you

can tell SPSS what kind of data you will be entering. The default value is a numeric field that is eight digits wide with two decimal places displayed. If your data are more than eight digits to the left of the decimal place, they will be displayed in scientific notation (e.g., the number 2,000,000,000 will be displayed as 2.00E+09). SPSS maintains accuracy beyond two decimal places, but all output will be rounded to two decimal places unless otherwise indicated in the *Decimal Places* blank.

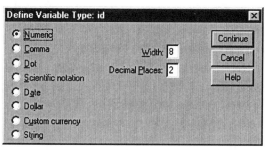

SPSS accepts a variety of data types. To learn more about each variable type, you can right-click (click the right mouse button) with the pointer over the variable type. This general procedure (right-clicking over part of the active window) works to get help with most SPSS functions and screens.

In our example, we will be using numeric variables, so you should now click *Continue*.

Practice Exercise

Create a data file for the two sample students and six variables presented in Example 1.2.1 above. Name your variables: ID, DAY, TIME, MORNING, GRADE, and WORK. You should code DAY as 1 = Mon/Wed/Fri, 2 = Tues/Thurs. Code TIME as 1 = morning, 2 = afternoon. Code MORNING as 0 = No, 1 = Yes. Code WORK as 0 = No, 1 = Part-Time, 2 = Full-Time. Be sure you enter variable labels for your different values.

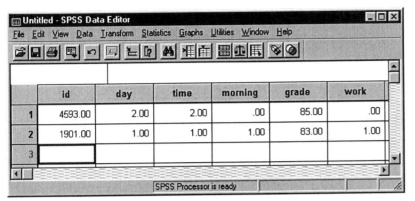

Be sure you enter the correct measurement scale type for each.

When done, you should have a data window that looks something like the window on the upper left. Notice that SPSS puts the variable names as column labels, and the cells contain the data as entered. This same Data Window can be changed to look something like the lower window to the left instead. Note that in this case the data cells display the variable labels that correspond to each value entered.

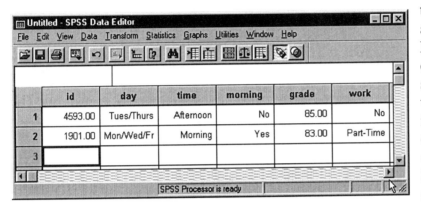

The two windows above represent two views of the same data. To toggle between the two views, you can click *Value Labels* under the *View* menu. You can also click the *Value Labels* icon on the toolbar (second from right in the windows above).

Section 1.4 Loading and Saving Data Files

Once you have entered your data, you will need to save it for later use, so that you can retrieve it when needed.

Loading and saving SPSS data files works in the same way as most Windows-based software. Under the FILE menu, there are OPEN and SAVE commands. SPSS data files have a .SAV extension (the extension is the last three letters of the file name; this tells Windows that it is an SPSS data file).

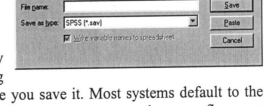

Save Your Data

When you save your data file (by clicking *File* then clicking *Save*, or by clicking on the disk icon), pay special attention to where you save it. Most systems default to the location <c:\program files\spss>. You will probably want to save your data on a floppy so that you can take the file with you, in which case you would select the location <a:\>.

Load Your Data

When you load your data (by clicking *File* then clicking *Open*, or by clicking the open file folder icon), you get a similar window. This window lists all files with the .SAV extension. If you have trouble locating your saved file, make sure you are looking in the right directory.

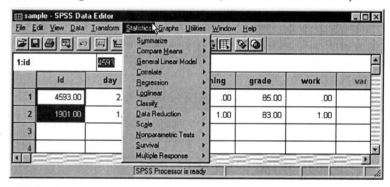

Practice Exercise

To be sure that you have mastered saving and opening data files, name your sample data file "sample" and save it on a floppy disk. Once saved, SPSS will display the name of the file at the top of the data window.

After you have saved your data, exit SPSS (by clicking on *File* then on *Exit*). Restart SPSS and load your data.

Section 1.5 Running Your First Analysis

Any time you open a data window, you can run any of the analyses available. To get started, let's calculate the students' average grade. (With only two students, you can easily check your answer by hand, but imagine a data file with 10,000 student records.)

The majority of the available statistical tests are under the *Statistics* menu. This menu displays all the options available for your version of the SPSS program. Other versions may have slightly different sets of options.

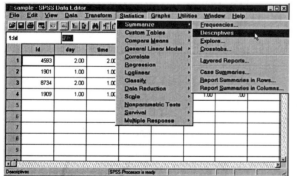

To calculate a **mean** (average) we are asking the computer to summarize our data set. Therefore, the command is run by clicking *Statistics*, then *Summarize*, then *Descriptives*.

This brings up the Descriptives dialog box shown on the next page. Note that the left side of the box contains a list of all of the variables in our data file. On the right is an area labeled *Variables* where we can select the variables we would like to use in the analysis.

6

In version 8.0, the Descriptives dialog box lists the variable labels (and names), along with an icon indicating the variable type. Earlier versions list just the variable names.

We want to compute the **mean** for the variable called GRADE. Thus, we need to select the variable name in the left window (by clicking on it). To transfer it to the right window, click on the arrow between the two windows. Note that double-clicking on the variable name will also transfer the variable to the right window, and this arrow can be used to transfer variables in either directions.

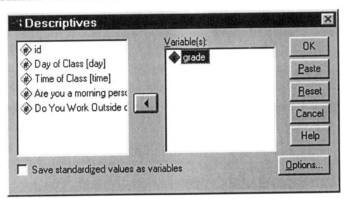

When we click on the *OK* button, the analysis will be conducted, and we will be ready to examine our output.

Section 1.6   Examining and Printing Output Files

After performing an analysis, your output is placed in the **output window,** and the output window becomes the active window. If this is the first analysis you have conducted since starting SPSS, then a new output window will be created. If you have run previous analyses and saved them, your output is added to the end of your previous output.

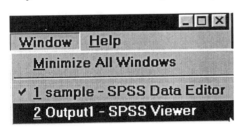

To switch back and forth between the data window and the output window, select the appropriate window using the *Window* menu bar.

The output window is split into two sections. The left section is an outline of the output (SPSS refers to this as the outline view). The right section is the output itself.

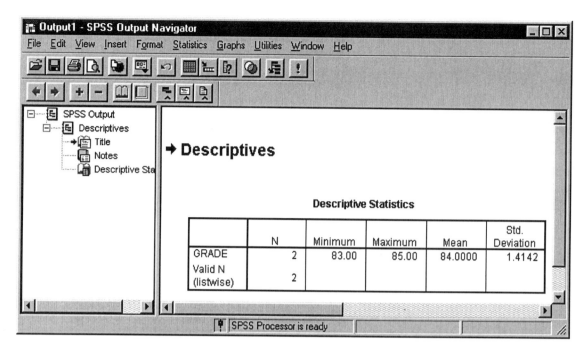

The section on the left of the output window provides an outline of the entire output window. All of the analyses are listed in the order in which they were conducted. Note that this outline can be used to quickly locate a section of the output. Simply click on the section you would like to see, and the right window will jump to the appropriate place.

Clicking on a statistical procedure also selects all of the output for that command. By pressing the *delete* key, that output can be deleted from the output window. This is a quick way to be sure that your output window contains only the output you want. Output can also be selected and pasted into a word processor by clicking *Edit* then *Copy* to copy the output. You can then switch to your word processor and click *Edit* then *Paste.*

To print your output, simply click *File* then *Print* or click on the printer icon on the toolbar. You will have the option of printing all of your output, or just the currently selected section. Be careful when printing! Each time you run a command, the output is added to the end of your previous output. Thus, you could be printing a very large output file containing information you may not want or need.

One way to ensure that your output window contains only the results of the current command is to create a new output window just before running the command. To do this, click *File* then *New* then *Output.* All your subsequent commands will go into your new output window.

Practice Exercise

Load the sample data file you created earlier (SAMPLE.SAV). Run the *Descriptives* command for the variable *GRADE* and print out the output. Your output should look like the example above. Next, select the data window and print it.

Section 1.7   Modifying Data Files

Once you have created a data file, it is really quite simple to add additional cases (rows/subjects) or additional variables (columns). Consider example 1.7.1.

Example 1.7.1

Two more students provide you with their surveys. Their information is:

Response Sheet 3
ID: 8734
Day of class: ____ MWF   _X_ TR
Class time: _X_ Morning   ____ Afternoon
Are you a morning person?   ____ Yes   _X_ No
Final grade in class: 80%
Do you work outside of school?   ____ Full-time   ____ Part-time
                                     _X_ No

Response Sheet 4
ID: 1909
Day of class: _X_ MWF   ____ TR
Class time: _X_ Morning   ____ Afternoon
Are you a morning person?   _X_ Yes   ____ No
Final grade in class: 73%
Do you work outside of school?   ____ Full-time   _X_ Part-time
                                     ____ No

To add these data, simply place two additional rows in the data window (after loading your sample data). Notice that as new subjects are added, the row numbers become bold.

You can also add new variables. For example, if the first two subjects were given special training on time management, and the two new subjects were not, you could change your data file to reflect this additional information. The new variable could be called TRAINING (whether or not the

subject received training), and it would be coded so that 0 = no training and 1= training. Thus, the first two subjects would be assigned a "1" and the last two subjects a "0". To do this, click *Data*, then click *Define Variable*, and follow the same procedure we used before to name the variable and label the values.

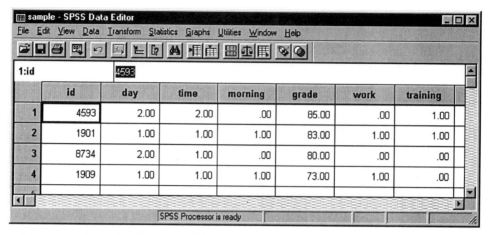

Adding data and adding variables are just logical extensions of the procedures we used when originally creating the data file. Save this new data file. We will be using it again later in the book.

Practice Exercise

Follow along with the example above. Make the modifications to your SAMPLE.SAV data file, and save it.

Chapter 2

Entering and Modifying Data

In Chapter 1, we learned how to create a simple data file, save it, perform a basic analysis, and examine the output. In this section, we will go into more detail about variables and data.

Section 2.1 Variables and Data Representation

In SPSS, variables are represented as columns in the data file. Subjects are represented as rows. Thus, if we collect 4 pieces of information from 100 subjects, we will have a data file with 4 columns and 100 rows.

Measurement Scales

There are four types of measurement scales: **nominal, ordinal, interval,** and **ratio.** While the measurement scale will determine which statistical technique is appropriate for a given set of data, SPSS generally does not discriminate. Thus, we start this section with a warning that if you ask it to, SPSS may conduct an analysis that may not be appropriate for your data. For a more complete description of these four measurement scales, consult your statistics text or the glossary in Appendix C.

Let's look at the sample data file we created in Chapter 1. We calculated a **mean** for the variable GRADE. GRADE was measured on a **ratio scale,** and the **mean** is an acceptable summary statistic (assuming that the distribution is normal).

We could have had SPSS calculate a **mean** for the variable TIME instead of GRADE. If we did, we would get the output presented here.

The output indicates that the average TIME was 1.25. Remember that TIME was coded as an ordinal variable (1 = morning class, 2 = afternoon class). Thus, the **mean** is not an appropriate statistic for an **ordinal scale,** but SPSS calculated it anyway. The importance of considering the type of data cannot be overemphasized. Just because SPSS will compute a statistic for you does not mean that

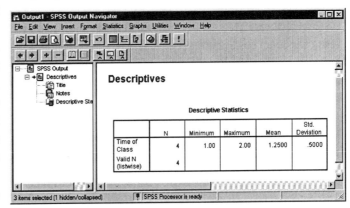

you should use it. Later in the text, when we discuss specific statistical procedures, the conditions under which they are appropriate will be discussed.

Missing Data

Often, participants do not provide complete data. For some students, you may have a pretest score but not a posttest score. Maybe one student left one question blank on a survey, or perhaps she didn't state her age. Missing data can weaken any analysis. Often, a

q1	q2	total
2.00	2.00	4.00
3.00	1.00	4.00
4.00	3.00	7.00
2.00	.	.
1.00	2.00	3.00

single missing question can eliminate a subject from all analyses.

If you have missing data in your data set, leave that cell blank. In the example to the left, the fourth subject did not complete Question 2. Note that the total score (which is calculated from the other two questions) is also blank because of the missing data for Question 2. SPSS represents missing data in the data window with a period (although you should not enter a period; just leave it blank).

Section 2.2   Transformation and Selection of Data

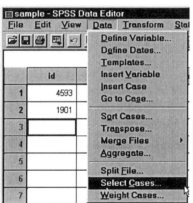

Often, we have more data in a data file than we want to include in a specific analysis. For example, our sample data file contains data from four subjects, two who received special training and two who did not. If we wanted to conduct an analysis using only the two subjects who did not receive the training, we would need to specify the appropriate subset.

Selecting a Subset

We can use the *Select Cases* command to specify a subset of our data. The *Select Cases* command is located under the *Data* menu. After selecting this command, the dialog box to the right will appear.

You can specify which cases (participants) you want to select by using the selection criteria on the right side.

By default, *All Cases* will be selected. The most common way to select a subset is to click *If condition is satisfied*, and then click on the button labeled *If*. This will bring up a new dialog box that will allow you to indicate which cases you would like to use.

You can enter the logic used to select the subset in the upper section. If the logical statement is true for a given case, then that case will be selected. If the logical statement is false, that case will not be selected. For example, you can select all cases that were coded as Mon/Wed/ Fri by entering the formula DAY=1 in the upper right part of the window. If DAY is 1, then the statement will be true, and SPSS will select the case. If DAY is anything other than 1, the statement will be false, and the case will not be selected. Once you have entered the logical statement, click on *Continue* to return to the Select Cases dialog box. Then, click on *OK* to return to the data window.

After selecting the cases, the data window will change slightly. The cases that were not selected will be marked with a diagonal line through the case number. For example, using our sample data, the first and third cases are not selected. Only the second and fourth cases are selected for this subset.

An additional variable will also be created in your data file. The new variable is called FILTER_$ and will indicate whether a case was selected or not selected.

If we calculate a **mean** GRADE using the subset we just selected we will receive the output to the right. Notice that we now have a **mean** of 78.00 with a sample size (*N*) of 2 instead of 4.

Descriptive Statistics

	N	Minimum	Maximum	Mean	Std. Deviation
GRADE	2	73.00	83.00	78.0000	7.0711
Valid N (listwise)	2				

Be careful when you select subsets. The subset remains in effect until you run the command again and select all cases. You can tell if you have a subset selected because the bottom of the data window will indicate that a Filter is on. In addition, when you examine your output, *N* will be less than the total number of records in your data set if a subset is selected. The diagonal lines through some cases will also be evident when a subset is selected.

Computing a New Variable

SPSS can also be used to compute a new variable or to manipulate your existing variables. To illustrate this, let's create a new data file. This file will contain data for four subjects and three variables (Q1, Q2, and Q3). The variables represent the number of points each subject received on three different questions. Now enter the data shown on the screen to the right. When done, save this data file as "QUESTIONS.SAV." We will be using it again in later chapters.

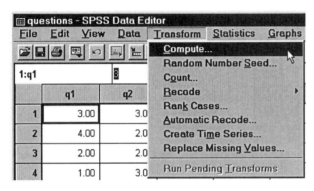

The blank marked *Target Variable* is where we enter the name of the new variable we want to create. In the example, we are creating a variable called TOTAL.

Notice that there is an equal sign between the Target Variable blank and the Numeric Expression blank. These two blank areas are the two sides of an equation that SPSS will

Now you will calculate the total score for each subject. We could do this manually, but if the data file were large, or if there were a lot of questions, this would take a long time. It is more efficient (and more accurate) to have SPSS compute the total for you. To do this, click on *Transform* and then click on *Compute*. After clicking in the Compute command, we get the dialog box below.

calculate. For example, TOTAL = Q1 + Q2 + Q3 is the equation that is entered in the sample presented here. Note that it is possible to create any equation here simply by using the number and operational keypad at the bottom of the dialog box. When we click on *OK*, SPSS will create a new variable called TOTAL and make it equal to the sum of the three questions.

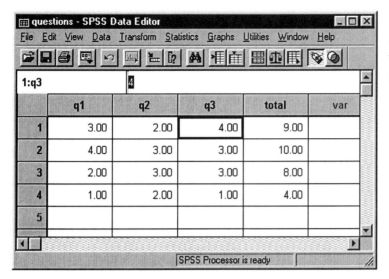

Save your data file again so that the new variable will be available for future sessions.

Recoding a Variable—Different Variable

SPSS can create a new variable based upon data from another variable. Let's say we want to split our subjects based upon their total score. We want to create a variable called GROUP, which is coded 1 if the total score is low (less than 8) or 2 if the total score

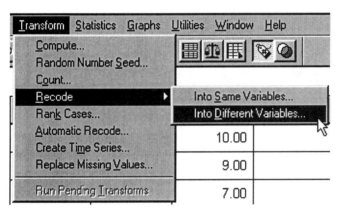

is high (9 or larger). To do this, we click *Transform*, then *Recode*, then *Into Different Variable*.

This will bring up the Recode into Different Variables dialog box shown below. Transfer the variable TOTAL to the middle blank. Enter GROUP as the *Name* of the output variable. Click *Change* and the middle blank will show that TOTAL is becoming GROUP.

15

Click *Old and New Values*. This will bring up the dialog box shown below. In this example, we have entered a 9 in the *Range through highest* and a 2 in the *New Value* area. When we click *Add*, the blank on the right displays the recoding formula. Now enter an 8 on the left in the *Range Lowest Through* blank, and a 1 in the *New Value* blank. Click *Add*, then *Continue*. Click *OK*. You will be returned to the data window. A new variable (GROUP) will have been added and coded as 1 or 2 based on TOTAL.

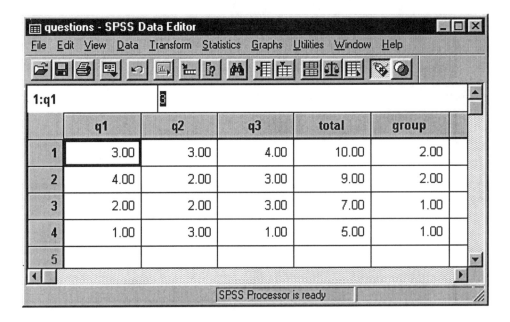

Chapter 3

Descriptive Statistics

In Chapter 2, we discussed many of the options available in SPSS for dealing with data. Now, we will discuss ways to summarize our data. The set of procedures used to describe and summarize data are called **descriptive statistics**.

Section 3.1   Frequency Distributions and Percentile Ranks for a Single Variable

Description

The *Frequencies* command produces frequency distributions for the specified variables. The output includes the number of occurrences, percentages, valid percentages, and cumulative percentages. The valid percentages and the cumulative percentages comprise only the data that are not designated as missing.

The *Frequencies* command is useful for describing samples where the **mean** is not useful (e.g., nominal or ordinal scales). It is also useful as a method of getting the "feel" of your data. It provides more information than just a **mean** and **standard deviation** and can be a useful means of determining **skew** and identifying **outliers**. One special feature of the command is its ability to determine **percentile ranks**.

Assumptions

Cumulative percentages and **percentiles** are valid only for data that are measured on at least an ordinal scale. Because the output contains one line for each value of a variable, this command works best on variables with a relatively small number of values.

Drawing Conclusions

The *Frequencies* command produces output that indicates both the number of cases in the sample of a particular value, and the percentage of cases with that value. Thus, conclusions drawn should relate only to describing the numbers or percentages of cases in the sample. If the data are at least ordinal in nature, conclusions regarding the cumulative percentage and/or percentiles can be drawn.

SPSS Data Format

The SPSS data file for obtaining frequency distributions requires only one variable. If you are using a **string variable** (a variable that contains letters as well as numbers), it must be only a few characters long, or it will not appear in the dialog box. For example, a string variable that contains a letter grade (A, B, C, D, or F) will work fine. A variable that contains the first name of each subject (and therefore is long and has a lot of possible values) will not work.

Creating a Frequency Distribution

To run the Frequencies command, click *Statistics,* then *Summarize,* then *Frequencies.* (This example uses the CARS.SAV data file that comes with SPSS. It is probably located at <c:\program files\spss\cars.sav>).

This will bring up the main dialog box. Transfer the variable for which you would like a frequency distribution into the Variables blank on the right. Be sure that the *Display frequency tables* option is checked. Click *OK* to receive your output.

Output for a Frequency Distribution

The output consists of two sections. The first section indicates the number of records with **valid data** for each variable selected. Records with a blank score are listed as missing. In the example below (obtained from the CARS.SAV data file), the data file contained 406 records. All of those contained data in the model year (YEAR) variable. Notice that the variable label is Model Year (modulo 100).

Statistics

Model Year (modulo 100)

N	Valid	406
	Missing	0

Model Year (modulo 100)

		Frequency	Percent	Valid Percent	Cumulative Percent
Valid	0	1	.2	.2	.2
	70	34	8.4	8.4	8.6
	71	29	7.1	7.1	15.8
	72	28	6.9	6.9	22.7
	73	40	9.9	9.9	32.5
	74	27	6.7	6.7	39.2
	75	30	7.4	7.4	46.6
	76	34	8.4	8.4	54.9
	77	28	6.9	6.9	61.8
	78	36	8.9	8.9	70.7
	79	29	7.1	7.1	77.8
	80	29	7.1	7.1	85.0
	81	30	7.4	7.4	92.4
	82	31	7.6	7.6	100.0
	Total	406	100.0	100.0	

The second section of the output (shown on the top) contains a cumulative frequency distribution for each variable selected. At the top of the section, the variable label is given. The output itself consists of five columns. The first column lists the values of the variable in sorted order. There is a row for each value of your variable, and additional rows are added at the bottom for the Total and missing data. The second column gives the frequency of each value, including missing values. The third column gives the percentage of all records (including records with missing data) for each value. The fourth column, labeled Valid Percent, gives the percentage of records (without including records with missing data) for each value. If there were any missing values, these values would be larger than the values in column three because the total number of records would have been reduced by the number of records with missing values. The final column gives cumulative percentages. Cumulative percentages indicate the percentage of records with a score equal to or smaller than the current value. Thus, the last value is always 100%. These values are equivalent to percentile ranks for the values listed.

Determining Percentile Ranks

The *Frequencies* command can be used to provide a number of descriptive statistics, as well as a variety of percentile values (including **quartiles**, cut points, and scores corresponding to a specific **percentile rank**).

To obtain either the descriptive or percentile functions of the *Frequencies* command, click the *Statistics* button at the bottom of the main dialog box.

This brings up the Frequencies: Statistics dialog box. Check any additional desired statistic by clicking on the blank next to it. For Percentiles, enter the desired percentile rank in the blank to the right of the *Percentiles* label. Then, click on *Add* to add it to the list of percentiles requested. Once you have selected all your required statistics, click *Continue* to return to the main dialog box.

Output for Percentile Ranks

The Statistics dialog box adds on to the previous output from the Frequencies command. The new section of the output is shown below.

The output contains a row for each piece of information you requested. In the example above, we checked *Quartiles* and asked for the 80th percentile. Thus, the output contains rows for the 25th, 50th, 75th, and 80th percentiles.

Statistics

Model Year (modulo 100)

N	Valid	406
	Missing	0
Percentiles	25	73.00
	50	76.00
	75	79.00
	80	80.00

Practice Exercise

Using Practice Data Set 1 in Appendix B, create a frequency distribution table for the mathematics skill scores. Determine the mathematics skill score at which the 60th percentile lies.

Section 3.2   Frequency Distributions and Percentile Ranks For Multiple Variables

Description

The *Crosstabs* command produces frequency distributions for multiple variables. The output includes the number of occurrences of each combination of levels of each variable. It is possible to have the command give percentages for any or all variables.

The *Crosstabs* command is useful for describing samples where the **mean** is not useful (e.g., nominal or ordinal scales). It is also useful as a method of getting a "feel" for your data.

Assumptions

Because the output contains a row or column for each value of a variable, this command works best on variables with a relatively small number of values.

SPSS Data Format

The SPSS data file for the *Crosstabs* command requires two or more variables. If you are using a **string variable**, it must be only a few characters long, or it will not appear in the dialog box.

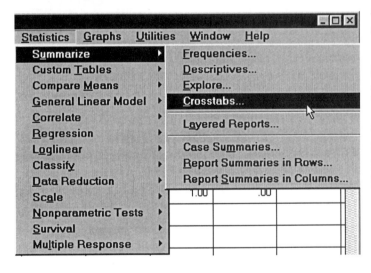

Running the Crosstabs Command

This example uses the SAMPLE.SAV data file, which you created in Chapter 1.

To run the procedure, click *Statistics*, then *Summarize*, then *Crosstabs*. This will bring up the main Crosstabs dialog box.

The dialog box lists all variables on the left, and contains two blanks labeled *Rows* and *Columns*. Enter one variable (TRAINING) in the *Rows* box. Enter the second (WORK) in the *Columns* box. If you have more than two variables, enter them in the third area (just under the *Layer* indicator).

The *Cells* button allows you to specify percentages and other information to be generated for each combination of values. Click on *Cells*, and you will get the box below.

For the example presented here, check *Row, Column,* and *Total* percentages. Then click *Continue*. This will return you to the Crosstabs dialog box. Click *OK* to run the analysis.

Interpreting Crosstabs Output

The output consists of a contingency table. Each level of WORK is given a column. Each level of TRAINING is given a row. In addition, a row is added for total, and a column is added for total.

Each cell contains the number of subjects (e.g., one subject received no training and does not work; two subjects received no training, regardless of employment status).

The percentages for each cell are also shown. Row percentages add up to 100% horizontally. Column percentages add up to 100% vertically.

receive special training * Do You Work Outside of Class Crosstabulation

| | | | Do You Work Outside of Class | | |
			No	Part-Time	Total
receive special training	No	Count	1	1	2
		% within receive special training	50.0%	50.0%	100.0%
		% within Do You Work Outside of Class	50.0%	50.0%	50.0%
		% of Total	25.0%	25.0%	50.0%
	Yes	Count	1	1	2
		% within receive special training	50.0%	50.0%	100.0%
		% within Do You Work Outside of Class	50.0%	50.0%	50.0%
		% of Total	25.0%	25.0%	50.0%
Total		Count	2	2	4
		% within receive special training	50.0%	50.0%	100.0%
		% within Do You Work Outside of Class	100.0%	100.0%	100.0%
		% of Total	50.0%	50.0%	100.0%

Practice Exercise

Using Practice Data Set 1 in Appendix B, create a contingency table using the *Crosstabs* command. Determine the number of subjects in each combination of the variables SEX and MARITAL. What percentage of subjects is married? What percentage of subjects is male and married?

Section 3.3   Measures of Central Tendency and Measures of Dispersion for a Single Group

Description

Measures of central tendency are values that represent a typical member of the sample or population. The three primary types are the **mean, median**, and **mode**. Measures of dispersion tell you the variability of your scores. The primary types are the **range** and **standard deviation** (or **variance**). Together, a measure of central tendency and a measure of dispersion provide a great deal of information about the entire data set.

We will discuss these measures of central tendency and measures of dispersion in the context of the *Descriptives* command. Note that many of these statistics can also be calculated using several other commands (e.g., the *Frequencies* command).

Assumptions

Each measure of central tendency and measure of dispersion has different assumptions associated with it. The **mean** is the most powerful measure of central tendency, and also has the most assumptions. For example, to calculate a **mean**, the data must be measured on an **interval** or **ratio scale**. In addition, the distribution should be normally distributed or, at least, not be highly skewed. The **median** requires at least ordinal data. Because the **median** indicates only the middle score (when scores are arranged from high to low) there are no assumptions about the shape of the distribution. The **mode** is the weakest measure of central tendency. There are no assumptions for the **mode**.

The **standard deviation** is the most powerful measure of dispersion, but it, too, has several requirements. It is a mathematical transformation of the **variance** (the **standard deviation** is the square root of the **variance**). Thus, if one is appropriate, the other is, too. The **standard deviation** requires data measured on an **interval** or **ratio scale**. In addition, the distribution should be normal. The **range** is the weakest measure of dispersion. To calculate a **range**, the variable must be at least ordinal. For **nominal data**, the entire frequency distribution should be presented as a measure of dispersion.

Drawing Conclusions

When stating a measure of central tendency, it should also be accompanied by a measure of dispersion. Thus, when reporting a **mean**, you should also report a **standard deviation**. When presenting a **median**, you should also state the **range**.

SPSS Data Format

Only one variable is required.

Running the Command

The _Descriptives_ command will be the command you use the most for obtaining measures of central tendency and measures of dispersion. This example uses the SAMPLE.SAV data file we have used in the previous chapters.

To run the command, click _Statistics_, then click _Summarize_, then _Descriptives_. This will bring up the main dialog box for the Descriptives command. Any variables you would like information about can be placed in the right blank by double clicking them or by selecting them and then clicking on the arrow.

By default, you will receive the _N_ (the number of cases/subjects), the **minimum** value, the **maximum** value, the **mean**, and the **standard deviation**. Note that some of these may not be appropriate for the type of data you have selected.

If you would like to change the default statistics that are given, click _Options_ in the main dialog box. You will be given the options dialog box presented here.

Remember that you can see a full description of any checkbox by right-clicking on the label. For example, in the dialog box to the right, we right-clicked on *Skewness* to get the description shown.

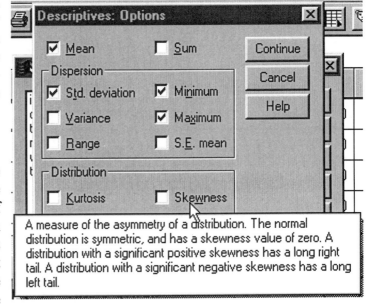

A measure of the asymmetry of a distribution. The normal distribution is symmetric, and has a skewness value of zero. A distribution with a significant positive skewness has a long right tail. A distribution with a significant negative skewness has a long left tail.

Reading the Output

The output for the *Descriptives* command is quite straightforward. Each type of output requested is presented in a column, and each variable is given in a row. The output presented here is for the sample data file. It shows that we have one variable (GRADE), and that we obtained the *N*, **minimum, maximum, mean,** and **standard deviation** for this variable.

Descriptive Statistics

	N	Minimum	Maximum	Mean	Std. Deviation
GRADE	4	73.00	85.00	80.2500	5.2520
Valid N (listwise)	4				

Practice Exercise

Using Practice Data Set 1 in Appendix B, obtain the descriptive statistics for the age of the subjects. What is the **mean**? The **median**? The **mode**? What is the **standard deviation**? **Minimum**? **Maximum**?

Section 3.4   Measures of Central Tendency and Measures of Dispersion for Multiple Groups

Description

The measures of central tendency discussed earlier are often needed not only for the entire data set, but also for several subsets. One way to obtain these values for subsets would be to use the data selection techniques discussed in Chapter 2, and to apply the *Descriptives* command to each subset. An easier way to perform this task is to use the *Means* command. The *Means* command is designed to provide descriptive statistics for subsets of your data.

Assumptions

The assumptions discussed in the section on Measures of Central Tendency and Measures of Dispersion for a Single Group (Section 3.3) also apply to multiple groups.

Drawing Conclusions

When reporting a measure of central tendency, it should also be accompanied by a measure of dispersion. Thus, when giving a **mean,** you should also report a **standard**

deviation. When presenting a **median**, you should also state the **range** or **interquartile range**.

SPSS Data Format

Two variables in the SPSS data file are required. One represents the **dependent variable** and will be the variable for which you receive the descriptive statistics. The other is the **independent variable** and will be used to create the subsets. Note that while SPSS calls this variable an **independent variable**, it may not meet the strict criteria necessary to be a true **independent variable** (e.g., physical manipulation). Thus, some SPSS procedures refer to it as the **grouping variable**.

Running the Command

The *Means* command is run by clicking *Statistics*, then *Compare Means* then *Means*.

This will bring up the main dialog box for the *Means* command. Place the selected variable in the blank labeled *Dependent List*.

Place the grouping variable in the box labeled *Independent List*. In this example, measures of central

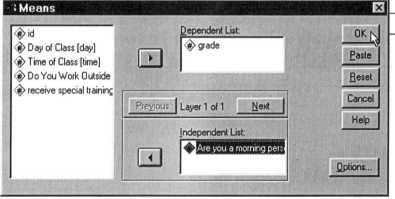

tendency and measures of dispersion for the variable GRADE will be given for each level of the variable MORNING.

By default, the **mean**, *N*, and **standard deviation** are given. If you would like additional measures, click on *Options* and you will be presented with the dialog box to the right. You can select any number of measures to be included.

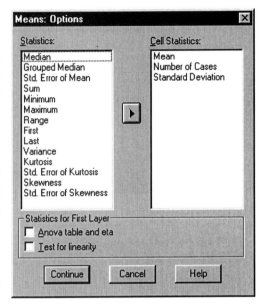

Reading the Output

The output for the *Means* command is split into two sections. The first section gives information about the data used, called a **case processing summary**. In our sample data file, there are four students (cases), and all of them were included in the analysis.

The second section of the output is the report from the *Means* command.

	Cases					
	Included		Excluded		Total	
	N	Percent	N	Percent	N	Percent
GRADE * Are you a morning person?	4	100.0%	0	.0%	4	100.0%

Report

GRADE

Are you a morning person?	Mean	N	Std. Deviation
No	82.5000	2	3.5355
Yes	78.0000	2	7.0711
Total	80.2500	4	5.2520

This report lists the name of the **dependent variable** at the top (GRADE). Every level of the **independent variable** is shown in a row in the table. In this example, the levels are 0 and 1, labeled No and Yes. Note that if a variable is labeled, the labels will be used instead of the raw values.

The summary statistics given correspond to the data, where the level of the **independent variable** is equal to the row heading (e.g., No, Yes). Thus, two subjects were included in each row.

An additional row is added, called Total. That row contains the combined data, and the values are the same as if we had run the *Descriptives* command for the variable GRADE.

Extension to More Than One Independent Variable

If you have more than one **independent variable**, SPSS can break down the output even further. Rather than adding more variables to the Independent List section of the dialog box, you need to add them in a different layer. Note that SPSS indicates which layer you are working with.

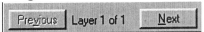

If you click *Next*, you will be presented with Layer 2 of 2, and you can select a second **independent variable** (e.g., TRAINING). Now, when you run the command (by clicking *OK*), you will be given summary statistics for the variable GRADE by each level of MORNING and TRAINING.

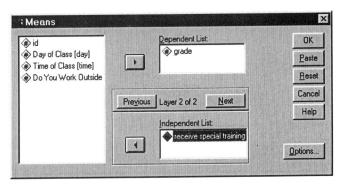

Your output will now look like the output below. You now have two main sections (No and Yes), along with the total. Now, however, each main section is broken down into subsections (No, Yes, and Total).

The variable you used in Level 1 (MORNING) is the first one listed and defines the main sections. The variable you had in Level 2 (TRAINING) is listed second. Thus, the first row represents those subjects who were not morning people and who did not receive training. The second row represents subjects who were not morning people and did receive training. The third row represents the total for all subjects who were not morning people.

Report

GRADE

Are you a morning person?	receive special training	Mean	N	Std. Deviation
No	No	80.0000	1	.
	Yes	85.0000	1	.
	Total	82.5000	2	3.5355
Yes	No	73.0000	1	.
	Yes	83.0000	1	.
	Total	78.0000	2	7.0711
Total	No	76.5000	2	4.9497
	Yes	84.0000	2	1.4142
	Total	80.2500	4	5.2520

Notice that **standard deviations** are not given for all of the rows. This is because there is only one subject per cell in this example. One problem with using many subsets is that it increases the required number of subjects to get meaningful results. See a research design text or your instructor for more details.

Practice Exercise

Using Practice Data Set 1 in Appendix B, compute the **mean** and **standard deviation** of ages for each value of marital status (e.g., what is the average age of the married subjects?).

Section 3.5 Standard Scores

Description

Standard scores allow the comparison of different scales by transforming the scores into a common scale. The most common standard score is the z-score. A z-score is based on a **standard normal distribution** (e.g., **mean** of 0 and a **standard deviation** of 1). A z-score, therefore, represents the number of **standard deviations** above or below the **mean** (e.g., a z-score of −1.5 represents a score 1½ **standard deviations** below the **mean**).

Assumptions

Z-scores are based on the **standard normal distribution**. Therefore, the distributions that are converted to z-scores should be normally distributed, and the scales should be either **interval** or **ratio**.

Drawing Conclusions

Conclusions based on z-scores consist of the number of **standard deviations** above or below the **mean**. For example, a student who scores 85 on a mathematics exam, with a class average of 70 and a **standard deviation** of 5, will have a z-score of 3.0 because she is three **standard deviations** above the **mean** (3 x 5 = 15). If the same student scores 90 on a reading exam, with a class **mean** of 80 and a **standard deviation** of 10, the z-score will be 1.0 because she is one **standard deviation** above the **mean**. Thus, even though her raw score was higher on the reading test, she actually did better on the mathematics test because her z-score was higher on that test.

SPSS Data Format

Calculating z-scores requires only a single variable in SPSS. That variable must be numerical.

Running the Command

Computing z-scores is a component of the *Descriptives* command. To access it, click *Statistics*, then *Summarize*, then *Descriptives*. This example uses the sample data file (SAMPLE.SAV) created in Chapter 1.

This will bring up the standard dialog box for the *Descriptives* command. Notice the checkbox in the bottom left corner labeled *Save standardized values as variables*.

Check this box and move the variable GRADE into the right-hand blank. Then, click *OK* to complete the analysis. You will be presented with the following output from the *Descriptives* command. Notice that the z-scores are not listed here. They were inserted into the data window as a new variable.

Descriptive Statistics

	N	Minimum	Maximum	Mean	Std. Deviation
GRADE	4	73.00	85.00	80.2500	5.2520
Valid N (listwise)	4				

Switch to the data window (by clicking on *Window*) and examine your data file. Notice that a new variable has been added, called ZGRADE. When you asked SPSS to save standardized values, it created a new variable, named the same as your old variable but preceded with a Z. The z-score is computed for each case and placed in the new variable.

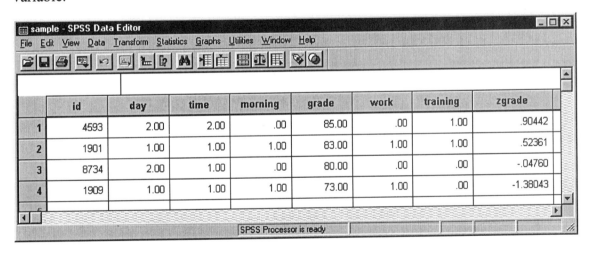

Reading the Output

After conducting your analysis, the new variable was created. You can perform any number of subsequent analyses on the new variable.

Practice Exercise

Using Practice Data Set 2 in Appendix B, determine the z-score that corresponds to each employee's salary. Determine the average z-score for salaries. Determine the mean z-score for salaries of male employees and female employees.

Notes

Chapter 4

Graphing Data

In addition to the frequency distributions and the measures of central tendency and measures of dispersion discussed in Chapter 3, graphing is a useful way to summarize, organize, and reduce your data. It has been said that a picture is worth a thousand words. In the case of complicated data sets, that is certainly true.

Unfortunately, graphing is one of the weaker functions of SPSS. The graphing capability is much improved in version 8.0, but it still leaves much to be desired. It is very difficult to make a publication-quality graph with SPSS. If you need a high quality graph, it is best to use a piece of graphing software (e.g., SigmaPlot) or a spreadsheet (e.g., Excel). For visualizing your data, however, SPSS makes graphs that are acceptable. One important advantage of using SPSS to create your graphs is that the data have already been entered. Thus, duplication is eliminated, and the chance of making a transcription error is reduced.

Editing SPSS Graphs

If you must use SPSS to create your graphs, you can edit them by right-clicking on the graph in the output window. Then, click *SPSS Chart Object*, then click on *Open*.

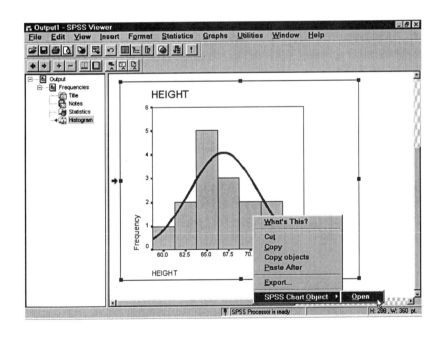

This will open the chart editing window. The chart editor allows you to alter the colors, fonts, and size of your graph.

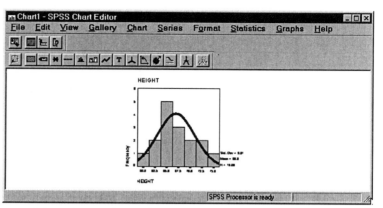

Data Set

For the graphing examples, we will use a new set of data. Enter the data below and save the file as HEIGHT.SAV. The data represent subjects' HEIGHT (in inches), WEIGHT (in pounds), and SEX (1 = male, 2 = female).

HEIGHT	WEIGHT	SEX
66	150	1
69	155	1
73	160	1
72	160	1
68	150	1
63	140	1
74	165	1
70	150	1
66	110	2
64	100	2
60	95	2
67	110	2
64	105	2
63	100	2
67	110	2
65	105	2

Check to be sure you have entered the data correctly by calculating a **mean** for each of the three variables (click *Statistics*, then *Summarize*, then *Descriptives*). Compare your results with those in the table below.

Descriptive Statistics

	N	Minimum	Maximum	Mean	Std. Deviation
HEIGHT	16	60.00	74.00	66.9375	3.9067
WEIGHT	16	95.00	165.00	129.0625	26.3451
SEX	16	1.00	2.00	1.5000	.5164
Valid N (listwise)	16				

Section 4.1   Bar Charts, Pie Charts, and Histograms

Description

Bar charts, pie charts, and histograms represent the number of times each score occurs by varying the height of a bar or the size of a pie piece. They are graphical representations of the frequency distributions discussed in Chapter 3.

Drawing Conclusions

The *Frequencies* command produces output that indicates both the number of cases in the sample with a particular value, and the percentage of cases with that value. Thus, conclusions drawn should relate only to describing the numbers or percentages for the sample. If the data are at least ordinal in nature, conclusions regarding the cumulative percentage and/or percentiles can also be drawn.

SPSS Data Format

Only one variable is needed to use this command.

Running the Command

The *Frequencies* command will produce graphical frequency distributions. Click *Statistics*, then click *Summarize*, then *Frequencies*. You will be presented with the main dialog box for the *Frequencies* command. (See Chapter 3 for other options available with this command.)

Click the *Charts* button at the bottom to produce frequency distributions. This will give you the Charts dialog box.

There are three types of charts available with this command: Bar Charts, Pie Charts, and Histograms. For each type, the *Y* axis can be either a frequency count or a percentage (selected with the *Chart Values* options).

You will receive the charts for any variables selected in the main Frequencies command dialog box.

Output

The bar chart consists of a *Y* axis representing the frequency, and an *X* axis representing each score. Note that the only values represented on the *X* axis are those values with non-zero frequencies (61, 62, and 71 are not represented).

HEIGHT Pie Chart

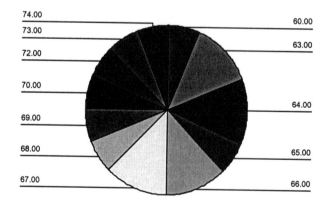

The pie chart shows the percentage of the whole that is represented by each value.

34

The Histogram creates a grouped frequency distribution. The range of scores is split into evenly spaced groups. The midpoint of each group is plotted on the *X* axis, and the *Y* axis represents the number of scores for each group. The Histogram also presents the **mean**, *N*, and **standard deviation**.

If you select *With Normal Curve*, a normal curve will be superimposed over the distribution. This is very useful for helping you

HEIGHT

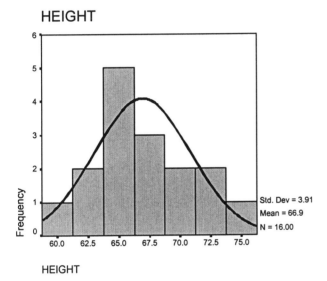

HEIGHT

determine if the distribution you have is approximately normal.

Practice Exercise

Use Practice Data Set 1 in Appendix B. After you have entered the data, construct a histogram that represents the mathematics skill scores and a bar chart that represents the frequencies for the variable AGES.

Section 4.2 Scatterplots

Description

Scatterplots (also called scattergrams or scatter diagrams) display two values for each case with a mark on the graph. The *X* axis represents the value for one variable. The *Y* axis represents the value for the second variable.

Assumptions

Both variables should be interval or ratio scales. If nominal or ordinal data are used, be cautious about your interpretation of the scattergram.

SPSS Data Format

Two variables are needed to perform this command.

Running the Command

Scatterplots can be produced by clicking *Graphs*, then *Scatter*. This will give you the first scatterplot dialog box. Select the desired Scatterplot (normally, you will select *Simple*) and click *Define*.

This will give you the main scatterplot dialog box. Enter one of your variables as the *Y* axis and the second as the *X* axis. For example, enter HEIGHT as the *Y* axis and WEIGHT as the X axis. Click on *OK*.

Output

The output will consist of a mark for each subject at the appropriate *X* and *Y* level.

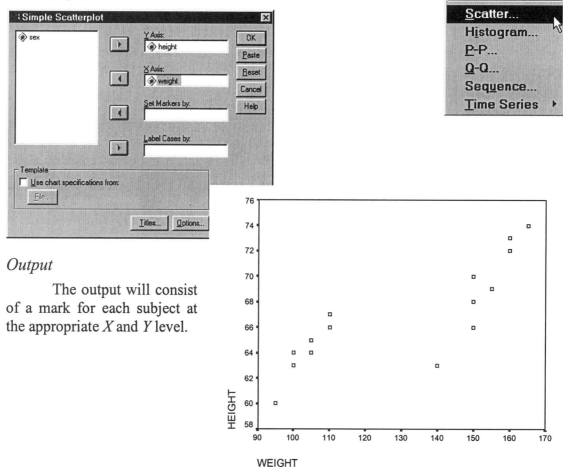

Adding a Third Variable

Even though the scatterplot is a two-dimensional graph, it is possible to have it plot a third variable. To do so, enter the third variable as the *Set Markers by* component. In our example, let's enter the variable SEX in the *Set Markers by* blank.

Now our output will have two different sets of marks. One set represents the Male subjects, and the second set represents the Female subjects. These two sets will be in two different colors on your screen.

Practice Exercise

Use Practice Data Set 2 in Appendix B. Construct a scatterplot to examine the relationship between SALARY and EDUCATION.

Section 4.3   Advanced Bar Charts

Description

Bar charts can be produced with the *Frequencies* command (see section 4.1 earlier in this chapter). Sometimes, however, we are interested in a bar chart where the *Y* axis is not a frequency. To produce such a chart, we need to use the bar charts command.

SPSS Data Format

At least two variables are needed to perform this command. There are two basic kinds of bar charts—between-subjects designs and repeated-measures designs. Use the between-subjects method if one variable is the **independent variable** and the other is the **dependent variable**. Use the repeated-measures method if you have a **dependent variable** for each value of the **independent variable** (e.g., you would have three variables for a design with three values of the **independent variable**).

Running the Command

Click *Graphs*, then *Bar* for either type of bar chart. This will open the bar chart dialog box. If you have one **independent variable**, select *Simple*. If you have more than one, select *Clustered*.

If you are using a between-subjects design, select *Summaries for groups of cases*. If you are using a repeated-measures design, select *Summaries of separate variables*.

If you are creating a repeated measures graph, you will see the dialog box below. Move each variable over to the *Bars Represent* area, and SPSS will place it inside parentheses following *Mean*. This will give you a graph like the one on the right below.

Practice Exercise

Use Practice Data Set 1 in Appendix B. Construct a bar graph examining the relationship between mathematics skill scores and marital status. Hint: In the *Bars Represent* area, enter SKILL as the variable.

Chapter 5

Prediction and Association

Section 5.1 Pearson Correlation Coefficient

Description

The Pearson correlation coefficient (sometimes called the Pearson product-moment correlation coefficient or simply the Pearson r) determines the strength of the linear relationship between two variables.

Assumptions

Both variables should be interval or ratio scale. If a relationship exists between them, that relationship should be linear. Because the Pearson correlation coefficient is computed using z-scores, both variables should also be normally distributed. If your data do not meet these assumptions, consider using the Spearman *rho* correlation coefficient instead.

SPSS Data Format

Two variables are required in your SPSS data file. Each subject must have data for both variables.

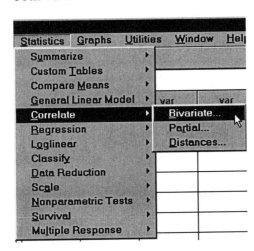

Running the Command

To select the Pearson correlation coefficient, click *Statistics*, then *Correlate*, then *Bivariate* (bivariate refers to two variables). This example uses the HEIGHT.SAV data file entered at the start of Chapter 4. This will bring up the main dialog box for Bivariate Correlations.

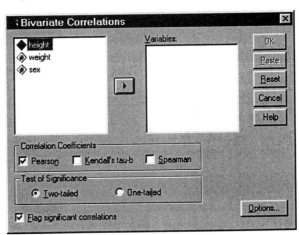

Move at least two variables from the box on the left to the right side by using the transfer arrow (or by double-clicking each variable). It is acceptable to move more than two variables. For our example, let's move all three variables over, and click *OK*.

Reading the Output

The output consists of a **correlation matrix**. Every variable you entered in the command is represented as both a row and a column. We entered three variables in our command. Therefore, we have a 3x3 table. There are also three rows in each cell—the correlation, the significance level, and the N.

Correlations

		HEIGHT	WEIGHT	SEX
HEIGHT	Pearson Correlation	1.000	.806**	-.644**
	Sig. (2-tailed)	.	.000	.007
	N	16	16	16
WEIGHT	Pearson Correlation	.806**	1.000	-.968**
	Sig. (2-tailed)	.000	.	.000
	N	16	16	16
SEX	Pearson Correlation	-.644**	-.968**	1.000
	Sig. (2-tailed)	.007	.000	.
	N	16	16	16

**. Correlation is significant at the 0.01 level (2-tailed).

The correlations are read by selecting a row and a column. For example, the correlation between height and weight is determined by selecting the WEIGHT row and the HEIGHT column (.806). We get the same answer by selecting the HEIGHT row and the WEIGHT column. The correlation between a variable and itself is always 1, so there is a diagonal set of 1.000s.

Drawing Conclusions

The correlation coefficient will be between −1.0 and +1.0. Coefficients close to 0 represent a weak relationship. Coefficients close to 1 or −1 represent a strong relationship. Significant correlations are flagged with asterisks. A significant correlation indicates a reliable relationship, not necessarily a strong correlation. With enough subjects, a very small correlation can be significant. Generally, correlations greater than .7 are considered strong. Correlations less than .3 are considered weak. Correlations between .3 and .7 are considered moderate. The same ranges apply to negative values.

Phrasing a Significant Result

In the example above, we obtained a correlation of .806 between HEIGHT and WEIGHT. A correlation of .806 is a strong positive correlation, and it is significant at the .007 level. Thus, we could state the following in a results section:

A Pearson correlation coefficient was calculated for the relationship between subjects' height and weight. A strong positive correlation was found ($r(14) =$ .806, $p < .01$), indicating a significant linear relationship between the two variables. Taller subjects tend to weigh more.

The conclusion states the direction (positive), strength (strong), value (.806), degrees of freedom (14), and significance level (< .01) of the correlation. In addition, a statement of direction is included (taller is heavier).

Note that the degrees of freedom given in parentheses is 14. The output indicates an N of 16. While most SPSS procedures give degrees of freedom, the correlation command gives only the N (the number of pairs). For a correlation, the degrees of freedom is $N − 2$.

Phrasing Results That Are Not Significant

Using our sample data set from the previous chapters, we could calculate a correlation between GRADE and ID. If so, we get the output on the right. The correlation has a significance level of .783. Thus, we could write the following in a results section:

Correlations

		ID	GRADE
ID	Pearson Correlation	1.000	.217
	Sig. (2-tailed)	.	.783
	N	4	4
GRADE	Pearson Correlation	.217	1.000
	Sig. (2-tailed)	.783	.
	N	4	4

A Pearson correlation was calculated examining the relationship between subjects' ID numbers and grades. A weak correlation that was not significant was found ($r(2) = .217$, $p > .05$). ID number is not related to grade in the course.

Practice Exercise

Use the data in Practice Data Set 2 in Appendix B. Determine the value of the Pearson correlation coefficient for the relationship between salary and years of education.

Section 5.2   Spearman Correlation Coefficient

Description

The Spearman correlation coefficient determines the strength of the relationship between two variables. It is a nonparametric procedure. Therefore, it is weaker than the Pearson correlation coefficient, but it can be used in more situations.

Assumptions

Because the Spearman correlation coefficient functions on the basis of the ranks of data, it requires ordinal (or interval or ratio) data for both variables. They do not need to be normally distributed.

SPSS Data Format

Two variables are required in your SPSS data file. Each subject must provide data for both variables.

Running the Command

Click *Statistics*, then *Correlate*, then *Bivariate*.

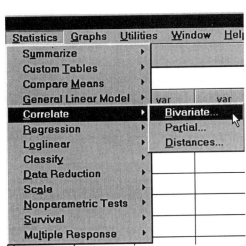

This will bring up the main dialog box for Bivariate Correlations (just like the Pearson correlation). About halfway down the dialog box is a section where you indicate the type of correlation you will compute. You can select as many as you want. For our example, remove the check in the *Pearson* box (by clicking on it), and click on the *Spearman* box. Use the variables HEIGHT and WEIGHT from our HEIGHT.SAV data file (see start of Chapter 4).

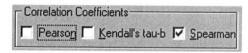

This is also one of the few commands that allow you to choose a one-tailed test.

Reading the Output

The output is essentially the same as for the Pearson correlation. Each pair of variables has its correlation coefficient indicated twice. The Spearman *rho* can range from −1 to +1 just like the Pearson *r*.

Correlations

			HEIGHT	WEIGHT
Spearman's rho	HEIGHT	Correlation Coefficient	1.000	.883**
		Sig. (2-tailed)	.	.000
		N	16	16
	WEIGHT	Correlation Coefficient	.883**	1.000
		Sig. (2-tailed)	.000	.
		N	16	16

**. Correlation is significant at the .01 level (2-tailed).

The output listed above indicates a correlation of .883 between HEIGHT and WEIGHT. Note the significance level of .000. This is, in fact, a significance level of < .001. The actual alpha level rounds out to .000, but it is not zero.

Drawing Conclusions

The correlation will be between −1.0 and +1.0. Scores close to 0 represent a weak relationship. Scores close to 1 or −1 represent a strong relationship. Significant correlations are flagged with asterisks. A significant correlation indicates a reliable relationship, but not necessarily a strong correlation. With enough subjects, a very small correlation can be significant. Generally, correlations greater than .7 are considered strong. Correlations less than .3 are considered weak. Correlations between .3 and .7 are considered moderate.

Phrasing Results That Are Significant

In the example above, we obtained a correlation of .883 between HEIGHT and WEIGHT. A correlation of .883 is a strong positive correlation, and it is significant at the .001 level. Thus, we could state the following in a results section:

A Spearman *rho* correlation coefficient was calculated for the relationship between subjects' height and weight. A strong positive correlation was found (*rho*(14) = .883, *p* < .001), indicating a significant relationship between the two variables. Taller subjects tend to weigh more.

The conclusion states the direction (positive), strength (strong), value (.883), degrees of freedom (14), and significance level (< .001) of the correlation. In addition, a statement of direction is included (taller is heavier). Note that the degrees of freedom given in parentheses is 14. The output indicates an *N* of 16.

Correlations

			ID	GRADE
Spearman's rho	ID	Correlation Coefficient	1.000	.000
		Sig. (2-tailed)	.	1.000
		N	4	4
	GRADE	Correlation Coefficient	.000	1.000
		Sig. (2-tailed)	1.000	.
		N	4	4

Phrasing Results That Are Not Significant

Using our sample data set from the previous chapters, we could calculate a Spearman *rho* correlation between GRADE and ID. If so, we would get the output on the left. The correlation coefficient equals 0.00 and has a significance level of 1.000. Note that this is rounded up and is not, in fact, 1.000. Thus, we could state the following in a results section:

A Spearman *rho* correlation coefficient was calculated for the relationship between a subject's ID number and grade. An extremely weak correlation that was not significant was found (*r*(2) = .000, *p* > .05). ID number is not related to grade in the course.

Practice Exercise

Use the data in Practice Data Set 2 in Appendix B. Determine the strength of the relationship between salary and job classification by calculating the Spearman *rho* correlation.

Section 5.3   Simple Linear Regression

Description

Simple linear regression allows the prediction of one variable from another.

Assumptions

Simple linear regression assumes that both variables are interval or ratio scaled. In addition, the **dependent variable** should be normally distributed around the prediction line. This, of course, assumes that the variables are related to each other linearly. Normally, both variables should be normally distributed. Dichotomous variables are also acceptable as **independent variables**.

SPSS Data Format

Two variables are required in the SPSS data file. Each subject must contribute to both values.

Running the Command

Click *Statistics*, then *Regression*, then *Linear*. This will bring up the main dialog box for linear regression. On the left side of the dialog box is a list of the variables in your data file (we are using the WEIGHT.SAV data file from the start of this section). On the right are blocks for the **dependent variable** (the variable you are trying to predict), and the **independent variable** (the variable we are predicting from).

We are interested in predicting someone's weight from his height. Thus, we should place the variable WEIGHT in the **dependent variable** block, and the variable HEIGHT in the **independent variable** block. Then, we can click *OK* to run the analysis.

Reading the Output

For simple linear regressions, we are interested in three components of the output. The first is called the Model Summary, and it occurs after the Variables Entered/Removed section. For our example, you should see this output. *R* Square (called the **coefficient of determination**) gives you the proportion of the variance of your **dependent variable** (WEIGHT) that can be explained by variation in your **independent variable** (HEIGHT). Thus, 64.9% of the variation in weight can be explained by differences in height (taller people weigh more).

Model Summary

Model	R	R Square	Adjusted R Square	Std. Error of the Estimate
1	.806[a]	.649	.624	16.1480

a. Predictors: (Constant), HEIGHT

The **standard error of estimate** gives you a measure of dispersion for your prediction equation. Using the prediction equation, 68% of the data will fall within one standard error of estimate of the predicted value. Just over 95% will fall within two standard errors. Thus, in the example above, 95% of the time, our estimated weight will be within 32.296 pounds of being correct (i.e., 2 x 16.148 = 32.296).

ANOVA[b]

Model		Sum of Squares	df	Mean Square	F	Sig.
1	Regression	6760.323	1	6760.323	25.926	.000[a]
	Residual	3650.614	14	260.758		
	Total	10410.938	15			

a. Predictors: (Constant), HEIGHT

b. Dependent Variable: WEIGHT

The second part of the output that we are interested in is the ANOVA summary table. More information on reading ANOVA summary tables will be given in Chapter 6. For now, the important number here is the significance level on the far right. If that value is less than .05, then we have a significant linear regression. If it is larger than .05, we do not.

The final section of the output is the table of coefficients. This is where the actual prediction equation can be found.

Coefficients[a]

Model		Unstandardized Coefficients		Standardized Coefficients	t	Sig.
		B	Std. Error	Beta		
1	(Constant)	-234.681	71.552		-3.280	.005
	HEIGHT	5.434	1.067	.806	5.092	.000

a. Dependent Variable: WEIGHT

In most texts, you learn that $Y' = a + bX$ is the regression equation. Y is your **dependent variable**, and X is your **independent variable**. In SPSS output, the values of both a and b are found in the B column. The first value, –234.681, is the value of a (and labeled constant). The second value, 5.434, is the value of b (and labeled with the name of the **independent variable**). Thus, our prediction equation for the example above is WEIGHT' = –234.681 + 5.434(HEIGHT). In other words, the average subject who is an inch taller than another subject weighs 5.434 more pounds. A person who is 60 inches tall should weigh –234.681 + 5.434(60) = 91.36 pounds. Given our earlier discussion of standard error of the estimate, 95% of people who are 60 inches tall will weigh between (91.36 – 32.30 = 59.06) and (91.36 + 32.30 = 123.66) pounds.

Drawing Conclusions

Conclusions from regression analyses indicate (a) whether or not a significant prediction equation was obtained, (b) the direction of the relationship, and (c) the equation itself.

Phrasing Results That Are Significant

In the example above, we obtained an R^2 of .649, and a regression equation of WEIGHT' = –234.681 + 5.434(HEIGHT). The ANOVA resulted in $F = 25.926$ with 1 and 14 degrees of freedom. The F is significant at the "less than .001" level. Thus, we could state the following in a results section:

> A simple linear regression was calculated predicting subjects' weight based on their height. A significant regression equation was found ($F(1,14) = 25.926$, $p < .001$), with an R^2 of .649. Subjects' predicted weight is equal to –234.68 + 5.43(height) pounds when height is measured in inches. Subjects' average weight increased 5.43 pounds for each inch of height.

The conclusion states the direction (increase), strength (.649), value (25.926), degrees of freedom (1,14), and significance level (< .001) of the regression. In addition, a statement of the equation itself is included.

Phrasing Results That Are Not Significant

If the ANOVA is not significant, the section of the output labeled *Sig* will be greater than .05, and the regression equation is not significant. A results section might include the following statement:

> A simple linear regression was calculated predicting subjects' ACT scores based on their height. The regression equation was not significant ($F(1,14) = 1.21$, $p > .05$) with an R^2 of .062. Height cannot be used to predict ACT scores.

Note that for results that are not significant, the ANOVA results and R^2 results are given, but the regression equation is not.

Practice Exercise

Use the data in Practice Data Set 2 in Appendix B. If we want to predict salary from years of education, what salary would you predict for someone with 12 years of education? What salary would you predict for someone with a college education (16 years)?

Section 5.4   Multiple Linear Regression

Description

The multiple linear regression analysis allows the prediction of one variable from several other variables.

Assumptions

Multiple linear regression assumes that all variables are interval or ratio scaled. In addition, the **dependent variable** should be normally distributed around the prediction line. This, of course, assumes that the variables are related to each other linearly.

Normally, all variables should be normally distributed. Dichotomous variables are also acceptable as **independent variables**.

SPSS Data Format

At least three variables are required in the SPSS data file. Each subject must contribute all values.

Running the Command

Click *Statistics*, then *Regression*, then *Linear*. This will bring up the main dialog box for linear regression. On the left side of the dialog box is a list of the variables in your data file (we are using the HEIGHT.SAV data file from the start of this section). On the right side of the dialog box are blanks for the **dependent variable** (the variable you are trying to predict) and the **independent variables** (the variables you are predicting from).

We are interested in predicting someone's weight based on their height and their sex. We believe that both a person's sex and her height influence weight. Thus, we should place the variable WEIGHT in the **dependent variable** block, and the variables HEIGHT and SEX in the Independent Variable block. Enter them both in Block 1.

This will perform an analysis to determine if WEIGHT can be predicted from SEX and/or HEIGHT. There are several methods SPSS can use to conduct this analysis. These can be selected with the *Method* box. Method *Enter* puts all variables in the equation whether they are significant or not, and is the most widely used. The other methods use various means to enter only those variables that are significant predictors. Click *OK* to run the analysis.

Reading the Output

For multiple linear regression, there are three components of the output that we are interested in. The first is called the Model Summary and is found after the Variables Entered/ Removed

Model Summary

Model	R	R Square	Adjusted R Square	Std. Error of the Estimate
1	.997[a]	.993	.992	2.2957

a. Predictors: (Constant), HEIGHT, SEX

section. For our example, you should get the output above. *R* Square (called the **coefficient of determination**) tells you the proportion of the variance in the **dependent variable** (WEIGHT) that can be explained by variation in the **independent variables** (HEIGHT and SEX in this case). Thus, 99.3% of the variation in weight can be explained by differences in height and sex (taller people weigh more, and men weigh more). Note that by adding a second variable, our R^2 goes up from .649 to .993. The .649 was obtained using the Simple Linear Regression example in Section 5.3.

The Standard Error of Estimate gives you a margin of error for the prediction equation. Using the prediction equation, 68% of the data will fall within one standard error of the estimate of the predicted value. Just over 95% will fall within two standard errors of the estimates. Thus, in the example above, 95% of the time, our estimated weight will be within 4.593 pounds of being correct. In our Simple Linear Regression example in Section 5.3, this number was 32.296. Note the higher degree of accuracy.

ANOVA[b]

Model		Sum of Squares	df	Mean Square	F	Sig.
1	Regression	10342.424	2	5171.212	981.202	.000[a]
	Residual	68.514	13	5.270		
	Total	10410.938	15			

a. Predictors: (Constant), HEIGHT, SEX

b. Dependent Variable: WEIGHT

The second part of the output that we are interested in is the ANOVA summary table. For more information on reading ANOVA tables, refer to the sections on ANOVA in Chapter 6. For now, the important number is the significance level on the far right. If that value is less than .05, then we have a significant linear regression. If it is larger than .05, we do not.

The final section of output we are interested in is the table of coefficients. This is where the actual prediction equation can be found.

Coefficients[a]

Model		Unstandardized Coefficients		Standardized Coefficients		
		B	Std. Error	Beta	t	Sig.
1	(Constant)	47.138	14.843		3.176	.007
	SEX	-39.133	1.501	-.767	-26.071	.000
	HEIGHT	2.101	.198	.312	10.588	.000

a. Dependent Variable: WEIGHT

In most texts, you learn that $Y' = a + bX$ is the regression equation. For multiple regression, our equation changes to $Y' = B_0 + B_1X_1 + B_2X_2 + \ldots + B_zX_z$ (where z is the number of Independent Variables). Y is your **dependent variable**, and the X's are your **independent variables**. The B's are listed in a column. Thus, our prediction equation for the example above is WEIGHT' = 47.138 – 39.133(SEX) + 2.101(HEIGHT) (where SEX is coded as 1 = Male, 2 = Female, and HEIGHT is in inches). In other words, the average difference in weight for subjects who are one inch different in height is 2.101 pounds. Males tend to weigh 39.133 pounds more than females. A female who is 60 inches tall should weigh 47.138 – 39.133(2) + 2.101(60) = 94.932 pounds. Given our earlier discussion of the standard error of estimate, 95% of females who are 60 inches tall will weigh between (94.932 + 4.593 = 90.339) and (94.932 + 4.593 = 99.525) pounds.

Drawing Conclusions

Conclusions from regression analyses indicate (a) whether or not a significant prediction equation was obtained, (b) the direction of the relationship, and (c) the equation itself. Multiple regression is generally much more powerful than simple linear regression. Compare our two examples.

With multiple regression, you must also consider the significance level of each Independent Variable. In the example above, the significance level of both **independent variables** is less than .001.

Phrasing Results That Are Significant

In our example, we obtained an R^2 of .993 and a regression equation of WEIGHT' = 47.138 – 39.133(SEX) + 2.101(HEIGHT). The ANOVA resulted in F = 981.20 with 2 and 13 degrees of freedom. That F is significant at the less than .001 level. Thus, we could state the following in a results section:

A multiple linear regression was calculated to predict subjects' weight based on their height and sex. A significant regression equation was found ($F(2,13)$ = 981.20, $p < .001$), with an R^2 of .993. Subjects' predicted weight is equal to 47.138 – 39.133(SEX) + 2.101(HEIGHT), when sex is coded as 1 = Male, 2 = Female, and height is measured in inches. Subjects increased 2.101 pounds for each inch of height, and males weighed 39.133 pounds more than females. Both sex and weight were significant predictors.

The conclusion states the direction (increase), strength (.993), value (981.20), degrees of freedom (2,13), and significance level (< .001) of the regression. In addition, a statement of the equation itself is included. Because there are multiple **independent variables**, we have noted whether or not each is significant.

Phrasing Results That Are Not Significant

If the ANOVA does not find a significant relationship, the *Sig* section of the output will be greater than .05, and the regression equation is not significant. A results section might include the following statement:

> A multiple linear regression was calculated predicting subjects' ACT scores based on their height and sex. The regression equation was not significant $(F(2,13) = 1.21, p > .05)$ with an R^2 of .062. Neither height nor weight can be used to predict ACT scores.

Note that for results that are not significant, the ANOVA results and R^2 results are given, but the regression equation is not.

Practice Exercise

Use the data in Practice Data Set 2 in Appendix B. Determine the prediction equation for predicting salary based on education, years of service, and sex. Which variables are significant predictors? If you believe that men were paid more than women, what would you conclude after conducting this analysis?

Chapter 6

Parametric Inferential Statistics

Parametric statistical procedures allow you to draw inferences about populations based on samples of those populations. To make these inferences, you must be able to make certain assumptions about the shape of the distributions of the population samples.

Section 6.1 Review of Basic Hypothesis Testing

The Null Hypothesis

In hypothesis testing, we create two hypotheses that are mutually exclusive (i.e., both cannot be true at the same time) and all inclusive, (i.e., one of them must be true). We refer to those two hypotheses as the **Null Hypothesis** and the **Alternative Hypothesis**. The null hypothesis generally states that any difference we observe is caused by random error. The alternative hypothesis generally states that any difference we observe is caused by a systematic difference between groups.

Type I and Type II Errors

All hypothesis testing attempts to draw conclusions about the real world based on the results of a test (a statistical test in this case). There are four possible combinations of results (see the figure below).

Two of the possible results are correct test results. The other two results are errors. A Type I error occurs when we reject a null hypothesis that is, in fact, true while a Type II error occurs when we fail to reject the null hypothesis when it is, in fact, false.

Significance tests determine the probability of making a Type I error. In other words, after performing a series of calculations, we obtain a probability that the null hypothesis is true. If there is a low probability such as 5 or less in 100 (.05), by convention, we reject the null hypothesis. In other words, we typically use the .05 level (or less) as the maximum Type I error rate we are willing to accept.

When there is a low probability of a Type I error such as .05, we can state that the significance test has led us to the decision to "reject the null hypothesis." This is synonymous with saying that a difference "is statistically significant." For example, suppose you found that a random sample of girls from a school district scored higher than a random sample of boys on a reading test. This result may have been obtained merely because the chance errors associated with random sampling created the observed difference (this is what the null hypothesis asserts). If there is a sufficiently low probability that random errors were the cause (as determined by a significance test), we can state that the difference between boys and girls is statistically significant.

Significance Levels vs. Critical Values

Most statistics textbooks present hypothesis testing by using the concept of a critical value. With such an approach, we obtain a value for a test statistic and compare it to a critical value we look up in a table. If the obtained value is larger than the critical value, then we reject the null hypothesis and conclude that we have found a significant difference (or relationship). If the obtained value is less than the critical value, then we fail to reject the null hypothesis and conclude that there is not a significant difference.

The critical value approach is well suited to hand calculations. Tables can be created that give critical values for alpha levels of .001, .01, .05, etc. It is not practical to create a table for every possible alpha level.

On the other hand, SPSS can determine the exact alpha level associated with any value of a test statistic. Thus, looking up a critical value in a table is not necessary. This does, however, change the basic procedure for determining whether or not to reject the null hypothesis.

The section of SPSS output labeled *Sig* (sometimes *p* or *alpha*) indicates the likelihood of making a Type I error if we reject the null hypothesis. A value of .05 or less indicates that we should reject the null hypothesis (assuming an alpha level of .05). A value greater than .05 indicates that we should fail to reject the null hypothesis.

In other words, when using SPSS, we (normally) reject the null hypothesis if the output value under *Sig* is equal to or smaller than .05 and fail to reject the null hypothesis if the output value is larger than .05.

One-Tailed vs. Two-Tailed Tests

SPSS output generally includes a two-tailed alpha level (it is normally labeled *Sig* in the output). A two-tailed hypothesis attempts to determine whether or not any difference (either positive or negative) exists. Thus, you have an opportunity to make a Type I error on either of the two tails of the normal distribution.

A one-tailed test examines a difference in a specific direction. Thus, we can only make a Type I error on one side (tail) of the distribution. If we have a one-tailed hypothesis, but our SPSS output gives a two-tailed significance result, we can take the significance level in the output and divide it by two. Thus, if our output indicates a significance level of .084 (two-tailed), but we have a one-tailed hypothesis, we can report a significance level of .042 (one-tailed).

Phrasing Results

Results of hypothesis testing can be stated in different ways, depending on the conventions specified by your institution. The following examples illustrate some of these differences.

Degrees of Freedom

Sometimes the degrees of freedom are given in parentheses immediately after the symbol representing the test, as in this example.

$$t(3) = 7.00, p < .01$$

Other times, the degrees of freedom are given within the statement of results.

$$t = 7.00, df = 3, p < .01$$

Significance Level

When you obtain results that are significant, they can be described in different ways. For example, if you obtained a significance level of .006 on a t test, you could describe it in any of the following three ways.

$$t(3) = 7.00, p < .05$$
$$t(3) = 7.00, p < .01$$
$$t(3) = 7.00, p = .006$$

Notice that since the exact probability is .006, both .05 and .01 are also correct.

There are also various ways of describing results that are not significant. For example, if you obtained a significance level of .505, any of the following three statements could be used.

$$t(2) = .805, ns$$
$$t(2) = .805, p > .05$$
$$t(2) = .805, p = .505$$

Statement of Results

Sometimes the results will be stated in terms of the null hypothesis, as in the following example.

The null hypothesis was rejected ($t = 7.00, df = 3, p = .006$).

Other times, the results are stated in terms of their level of significance.

A statistically significant difference was found: $t(3) = 7.00, p < .01$.

Statistical Symbols

Generally, statistical symbols are presented in *italics*. Prior to the widespread use of computers and desktop publishing, statistical symbols were underlined. Underlining is a signal to a printer that the highlighted text should be set in italics. Institutions vary on their requirements for student work, so you are advised to consult your instructor about this. You will notice that statistical symbols are underlined in the output from SPSS, but they are italicized in the text of this book.

Section 6.2   Single Sample *t* test

Description

The single sample *t* test compares the mean of a single sample to a known population mean. It is useful for determining if the current set of data has changed from a long term value (e.g., comparing the current year's temperatures to a historical average to determine if global warming is occurring).

Assumptions

The distributions from which the scores are taken should be normally distributed. However, the *t* test is robust and can handle violations of the assumption of a normal distribution. The **dependent variable** must be measured on an interval or ratio scale.

SPSS Data Format

The SPSS data file for the single sample *t* test requires a single variable in SPSS. That variable represents the set of scores in the sample that we will compare to the population mean.

Running the Command

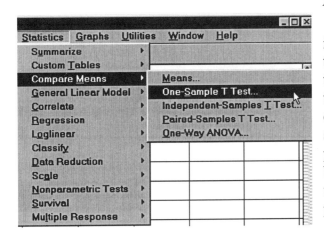

The single sample *t* test is located in the *Compare Means* submenu, under the *Statistics* menu. The dialog box for the single sample *t* test requires that we transfer the variable representing the current set of scores to the Test Variables section. We must also enter the population average in the *Test Value* blank. The example presented here is testing the variable LENGTH against a population mean of 35.

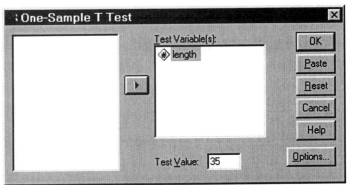

Reading the Output

The output for the single sample t test consists of two sections. The first section lists the sample variable and some basic descriptive statistics (N, mean, standard deviation, and standard error).

T-Test

One-Sample Statistics

	N	Mean	Std. Deviation	Std. Error Mean
LENGTH	10	35.9000	1.1972	.3786

One-Sample Test

	Test Value = 35					
					95% Confidence Interval of the Difference	
	t	df	Sig. (2-tailed)	Mean Difference	Lower	Upper
LENGTH	2.377	9	.041	.9000	4.356E-02	1.7564

The second section of output contains the results of the t test. The example presented here indicates a t value of 2.377, with 9 degrees of freedom and a significance level of .041. The mean difference of .9000 is the difference between the sample average (35.90) and the population average we entered in the dialog box to conduct the test (35.00).

Drawing Conclusions

The t test assumes an equality of means. Therefore, a significant result indicates that the sample mean is not equivalent to the population mean (hence the term "significantly different"). A result that is not significant means that there is not a significant difference between the means. It does not mean that they are equal. Refer to your statistics text for the section on failure to reject the null hypothesis.

Phrasing Results That Are Significant

The above example found a significant difference between the population mean and the sample mean. Thus, we could state the following:

A single sample t test compared the mean length of the sample to a population value of 35. A significant difference was found ($t(9) = 2.377, p < .05$). The sample mean of 35.90 ($sd = 1.197$) was significantly greater than the population mean.

Phrasing Results That Are Not Significant

If the significance level had been greater than .05, the difference would not be significant. If that had occurred, we could state the following:

A single sample *t* test compared the mean temperature over the past year to the long-term average. The difference was not significant ($t(364) = .54$, $p > .05$). The mean temperature over the past year was 67.8 ($sd = 1.4$) compared to the long-term average of 67.4.

Practice Exercise

The average salary in the U.S. is $25,000. Determine if the average salary of the subjects in Practice Data Set 2 (Appendix B) is significantly greater than this value. Note that this is a one-tailed hypothesis.

Section 6.3   The Independent Samples *t* test

Description

The independent *t* test compares the means of two samples. The two samples are normally from randomly assigned groups.

Assumptions

The two groups being compared should be independent of each other. Observations are independent when information about one is unrelated to the other. Normally, this means that one group of subjects provides data for one sample and a different group of subjects provides data for the other sample (and individuals in one group are not matched with individuals in the other group). One way to accomplish this is through random assignment to form two groups.

The scores should be normally distributed, but the *t* test is **robust** and can handle violations of the assumption of a normal distribution.

The **dependent variable** must be measured on an interval or ratio scale. The **independent variable** should have only two **discrete** levels.

SPSS Data Format

The SPSS data file for the independent *t* test requires two variables. One variable, the grouping variable, represents the value of the **independent variable**. The grouping variable should have two distinct values (e.g., 0 for a control group and 1 for an experimental group). The second variable represents the **dependent variable** such as scores on a test.

Conducting an Independent Samples t test

For our example, we will use the SAMPLE.SAV data file.

Click *Statistics*, then *Compare Means*, then *Independent Samples T Test*. This will bring up the main dialog box. Transfer the **Dependent Variable(s)** into the Test Variable

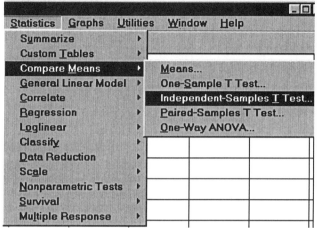

blank. For our example, we will use the variable GRADE.

Transfer the **independent variable** into the Grouping Variable section. For our example we will use the variable MORNING.

Next, click *Define Groups* and enter the values of the two levels of the **independent variable**. Independent *t* tests are only capable of comparing two levels at a time. Click *Continue* and then *OK* to run the analysis.

Output from the Independent Samples t test

The output will have a section labeled "Group Statistics." This section provides the basic descriptive statistics for the **Dependent Variable(s)** for each value of the **independent variable**. It should look like the output below.

Group Statistics

	Are you a morning	N	Mean	Std. Deviation	Std. Error Mean
GRADE	No	2	82.5000	3.5355	2.5000
	Yes	2	78.0000	7.0711	5.0000

Next, there will be a section with the results of the *t* test. It should look like the output below.

Independent Samples Test

		Levene's Test for Equality of Variances		t-test for Equality of Means					95% Confidence Interval of the Mean	
		F	Sig.	t	df	Sig. (2-tailed)	Mean Difference	Std. Error Difference	Lower	Upper
GRADE	Equal variances assumed	.	.	.805	2	.505	4.5000	5.5902	-19.5526	28.5526
	Equal variances not assumed			.805	1.471	.530	4.5000	5.5902	-30.0926	39.0926

The three columns labeled *t*, *df*, and *sig* provide the standard "answer" for the *t* test. They provide the value of *t*, the degrees of freedom (number of subjects, minus 2 in this case), and the significance level (often called *p*).

Drawing Conclusions

Recall from the previous section that the *t* test assumes an equality of means. Therefore, a significant result indicates that the means are not equivalent. When drawing conclusions about a *t* test, you must state the direction of the difference (i.e., which mean was larger than the other). You should also include information about the value of *t*, the degrees of freedom, the significance level, and the means and standard deviations for the two groups.

Phrasing Results That Are Significant

For a significant *t* test, you might state the following:

An independent *t* test comparing the mean scores of the experimental and control groups found a significant difference between the means of the two groups ($t(34) = 4.34$, $p < .05$). The mean of the experimental group was significantly higher ($m = 3.45$, $sd = .15$) than the mean of the control group ($m = 2.89$, $sd = .20$).

Phrasing Results That Are Not Significant

In our example above, we compared the scores of the morning people to the scores of the nonmorning people. We did not find a significant difference, so we could state the following:

An independent *t* test was calculated comparing the mean score of subjects who identified themselves as morning people to the mean score of subjects who did not identify themselves as morning people. No significant difference was found ($t(2) = .805$, $p > .05$). The mean of the morning people ($m = 78$, $sd = 7.07$) was not significantly different from the mean of nonmorning people ($m = 82.5$, $sd = 3.54$).

Practice Exercise

Use Practice Data Set 1 (Appendix B) to solve this problem. We believe that young people have lower mathematics skills than older people. We would test this hypothesis by comparing subjects 25 or younger (the "young" group) with subjects 26 or older (the "old" group). Hint: You may need to create a new variable; see Chapter 2 for help.

Section 6.4   Paired Samples *t* test

Description

The paired samples *t* test (also called a dependent *t* test) compares the means of two scores from related samples. For example, comparing a pretest and a posttest score for a group of subjects would require a paired samples *t* test.

Assumptions

The paired samples *t* test assumes that both variables are at the interval or ratio levels, and that they are normally distributed. The two variables should also be measured with the same scale. If the scales are different, the scores should be converted to *z*-scores before conducting the *t* test.

SPSS Data Format

Two variables in the SPSS data file are required. These variables should represent two measurements from each subject.

Running the Command

We will create a new data file containing five variables: PRETEST, MIDTERM, FINAL, INSTRUCT, and REQUIRED. INSTRUCT represents three different instructors for a course. REQUIRED represents whether the course was required or an elective (0 = elective, 1 = required). The other three variables represent exam scores (out of 100).

PRETEST	MIDTERM	FINAL	INSTRUCT	REQUIRED
56	64	69	1	0
79	91	89	1	0
68	77	81	1	0
59	69	71	1	1
64	77	75	1	1
74	88	86	1	1
73	85	86	1	1
47	64	69	2	0
78	98	100	2	0
61	77	85	2	0
68	86	93	2	1
64	77	87	2	1
53	67	76	2	1
71	85	95	2	1
61	79	97	3	0
57	77	89	3	0
49	65	83	3	0

Continued on next page

Continued

71	93	100	3	1
61	83	94	3	1
58	75	92	3	1
58	74	92	3	1

Enter the data and save it as GRADES.SAV. You can check your data entry by computing a mean for each instructor using the *Means* command (see Chapter 3 for more information). Use INSTRUCT as the **independent variable** and enter PRETEST, MIDTERM, and FINAL as your **dependent variables**.

Once you have the data entered, conduct a paired samples *t* test comparing pretest scores and final scores.

Report

INSTRUCT		PRETEST	MIDTERM	FINAL
1.00	Mean	67.5714	78.7143	79.5714
	N	7	7	7
	Std. Deviation	8.3837	9.9451	7.9552
2.00	Mean	63.1429	79.1429	86.4286
	N	7	7	7
	Std. Deviation	10.6055	11.7108	10.9218
3.00	Mean	59.2857	78.0000	92.4286
	N	7	7	7
	Std. Deviation	6.5502	8.6217	5.5032
Total	Mean	63.3333	78.6190	86.1429
	N	21	21	21
	Std. Deviation	8.9294	9.6617	9.6348

Click *Statistics*, then *Compare Means*, then *Paired Samples T Test*. This will bring up the main dialog box.

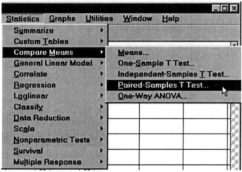

You must select pairs of variables to compare. As you select them, they are placed in the *Paired Variables* area.

Click once on PRETEST and then once on FINAL. Both variables will be moved into the *Current Selections* area. Click on the right arrow to transfer the pair to the *Paired Variables* section. Click *OK* to conduct the test.

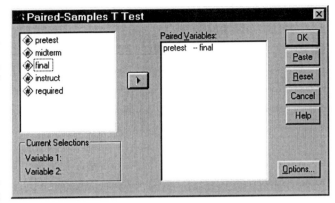

Reading the Output

The output for the paired samples *t* test consists of three components. The first part gives you basic descriptive statistics for the pair of variables. The PRETEST average was 63.3, with a standard deviation of 8.93. The FINAL average was 86.14, standard deviation 9.63.

Paired Samples Statistics

		Mean	N	Std. Deviation	Std. Error Mean
Pair 1	PRETEST	63.3333	21	8.9294	1.9485
	FINAL	86.1429	21	9.6348	2.1025

Paired Samples Correlations

		N	Correlation	Sig.
Pair 1	PRETEST & FINAL	21	.535	.013

The second part of the output is a Pearson correlation coefficient for the pair of variables.

Third, the section called *Paired Differences* contains information about the differences between the two variables. You may have learned in your statistics class that the paired samples *t* test is essentially a single sample *t* test calculated on the differences between the scores. The final three columns contain the value of *t*, the degrees of freedom, and the probability level. In the example presented here, we obtained a *t* of –11.646, with 20 degrees of freedom and a significance level of less than .001. Note that this is a two-tailed significance level. See the start of Chapter 6 for more details if you want to compute a one-tailed test.

Paired Samples Test

		Paired Differences							
					95% Confidence Interval of the Difference				
		Mean	Std. Deviation	Std. Error Mean	Lower	Upper	t	df	Sig. (2-tailed)
Pair 1	PRETEST - FINAL	-22.8095	8.9756	1.9586	-26.8952	-18.7239	-11.646	20	.000

Drawing Conclusions

Paired samples *t* tests determine whether or not two scores are significantly different from each other. Significant values indicate the two scores are different. Values that are not significant indicate the scores are not significantly different.

Phrasing Results That Are Significant

When stating the results of a paired samples *t* test, you should give the value of *t*, the degrees of freedom, and the significance level. You should also give the mean and standard deviation for each variable, as well as a statement of results that indicates whether you conducted a one- or two-tailed test.

Our example above was significant, so we could state the following:

> A paired samples *t* test was calculated to compare the mean pretest score to the mean final exam score. The mean on the pretest was 63.3 (*sd* = 8.93) and the mean on the posttest was 86.14 (*sd* = 9.63). A significant increase from pretest to posttest was found ($t(20) = 11.646, p < .001$).

Phrasing Results That Are Not Significant

If the significance level had been greater than .05 (or greater than .10 if you were conducting a one-tailed test), the result would not have been significant. For example, if *t* had been 1.50, the significance level would have been larger than .05, and we could state the following:

> A paired samples *t* test was calculated to compare the mean pretest score to the mean final exam score. The mean on the pretest was 63.3 (*sd* = 8.93) and the mean on the posttest was 86.14 (*sd* = 9.63). No significant difference from pretest to posttest was found ($t(20) = 1.50, p > .05$).

Practice Exercise

Use the same GRADES.SAV data file, and compute a paired samples *t* test to determine if scores increase from midterm to final.

Section 6.5   One-Way ANOVA

Description

Analysis of variance (ANOVA) is a procedure that determines the proportion of variability attributed to each of several components. It is one of the most useful and adaptable statistical techniques available.

The one-way ANOVA compares the means of two or more groups of subjects that vary on a single **independent variable** (thus the *one*-way designation). When we have three groups, we could use a *t* test to determine differences between groups, but we would have to conduct three *t* tests (Group 1 compared to Group 2; Group 1 compared to Group 3; and Group 2 compared to Group 3). When we conduct multiple *t* tests, we **inflate the Type I error rate** and increase our chance of drawing an inappropriate conclusion.

ANOVA compensates for these multiple comparisons and gives us a single answer that tells us if any of the groups is different from any of the other groups.

Assumptions

The One-Way ANOVA requires a single **dependent variable** and a single **independent variable**. Which group subjects belong to is determined by the value of the **independent variable**. Groups should be independent of each other. If our subjects belong to more than one group each, we will have to conduct a repeated measures ANOVA. If we have more than one **independent variable**, we would conduct a factorial ANOVA.

ANOVA also assumes that the **dependent variable** is at the interval or ratio levels, and normally distributed.

SPSS Data Format

Two variables are required in the SPSS data file. One variable serves as the **dependent variable** and the other as the **independent variable**. Each subject should provide only one score for the **dependent variable**.

Running the Command

For this example, we will use the GRADES.SAV data file we created in the previous section.

To conduct a one-way ANOVA, click *Statistics*, then *Compare Means*, then *One Way ANOVA*. This will bring up the main dialog box for the One-Way ANOVA command.

You should place the **independent variable** in the *Factor* box. For our example, INSTRUCT represents three different instructors, and it will be used as our **independent variable**.

Our **dependent variable** will be FINAL. This test will allow us to determine if the instructor has any effect on final grades in the course.

Click on the *Options* box to get the options dialog box. Click *Descriptive*. This will give you means for the **dependent variable** at each level of the **independent variable**. Checking this box here prevents us from having to run a separate means command. Click *Continue* to return to the main dialog box. Next, click *Post-Hoc* to bring up the Post Hoc Multiple Comparisons box. Click *Tukey*, and click *Continue*.

Post-hoc tests are necessary in the event of a significant ANOVA. The ANOVA indicates only if any group is different from any other group. If it is significant, we need to determine which groups are different from which other groups. We could do *t* tests to determine that, but we would have the same problem as before with inflating the Type I error rate.

There are a variety of post-hoc comparisons available that correct for the multiple comparisons. The most widely used is Tukey's HSD. SPSS will calculate a variety of post-hoc tests for you. Consult an advanced statistics text for a discussion of the differences between these various tests.

Now click *OK* to run the analysis.

Reading the Output

Descriptive statistics will be given for each instructor (i.e., level of the **independent variable**) and the total.

Descriptives

			N	Mean	Std. Deviation	Std. Error	95% Confidence Interval for Mean Lower Bound	95% Confidence Interval for Mean Upper Bound	Minimum	Maximum
FINAL	INSTRUCT	1.00	7	79.5714	7.9552	3.0068	72.2141	86.9288	69.00	89.00
		2.00	7	86.4286	10.9218	4.1281	76.3276	96.5295	69.00	100.00
		3.00	7	92.4286	5.5032	2.0800	87.3389	97.5182	83.00	100.00
		Total	21	86.1429	9.6348	2.1025	81.7572	90.5285	69.00	100.00

ANOVA

		Sum of Squares	df	Mean Square	F	Sig.
FINAL	Between Groups	579.429	2	289.714	4.083	.034
	Within Groups	1277.143	18	70.952		
	Total	1856.571	20			

The next section of the output is the ANOVA source table. This is where the various components of the variance have been listed, along with their relative sizes. For a one-way ANOVA there are two components to the variance: Between Groups (which represents the differences due to our **independent variable**) and Within Groups (which represents differences within each level of our **independent variable**). For our example, the Between Groups variance represents differences due to different instructors. The Within Groups variance represents individual differences in students.

The primary answer is *F*. *F* is a ratio of explained variance to unexplained variance. Consult a statistics text for more details on how it is determined. The *F* has two different degrees of freedom, one for Between Groups (in this case, 2 is the number of levels of our **independent variable**, minus 1) and one for Within Groups (18 is the number of subjects minus the number of levels of our **independent variable**).

The next part of the output consists of the results of our Tukey's HSD post-hoc comparison.

Multiple Comparisons

Dependent Variable: FINAL

Tukey HSD

(I) INSTRUCT	(J) INSTRUCT	Mean Difference (I-J)	Std. Error	Sig.	95% Confidence Interval	
					Lower Bound	Upper Bound
1.00	2.00	-6.8571	4.502	.304	-18.3482	4.6339
	3.00	-12.8571*	4.502	.027	-24.3482	-1.3661
2.00	1.00	6.8571	4.502	.304	-4.6339	18.3482
	3.00	-6.0000	4.502	.396	-17.4911	5.4911
3.00	1.00	12.8571*	4.502	.027	1.3661	24.3482
	2.00	6.0000	4.502	.396	-5.4911	17.4911

*. The mean difference is significant at the .05 level.

This table presents us with every possible combination of levels of our **independent variable**. The first row represents Instructor 1 compared to Instructor 2. Next is Instructor 1 compared to Instructor 3. Next is Instructor 2 compared with Instructor 1 (note that this is redundant with the first row). Next is Instructor 2 compared with Instructor 3, and so on.

The column labeled *sig* represents the Type I error (*p*) rate for the simple (2 level) comparison in that row. In our example above, Instructor 1 is significantly different from

Instructor 3, but Instructor 1 is not significantly different from Instructor 2, and Instructor 2 is not significantly different from Instructor 3.

Drawing Conclusions

Drawing conclusions for ANOVA requires that we indicate the value of F, two degrees of freedom, and the significance level. A significant ANOVA should be followed by the results of a post-hoc analysis and a verbal statement of the results.

Phrasing Results That Are Significant

In our example above, we could state the following:

We computed a one-way ANOVA comparing the final exam scores of subjects who took a course from one of three different instructors. A significant difference was found among the instructors ($F(2,18) = 4.08$, $p < .05$). Tukey's HSD was used to determine the nature of the differences between the instructors. This analysis revealed that students who had instructor 1 scored higher ($m = 79.57$, $sd = 7.96$) than students who had instructor 3 ($m = 92.43$, $sd = 5.50$). Students who had instructor 2 ($m = 86.43$, $sd = 10.92$) were not significantly different from either of the other two groups.

Phrasing Results That Are Not Significant

If we had conducted the analysis using PRETEST as our **dependent variable** instead of FINAL, we would have received the following output:

ANOVA

		Sum of Squares	df	Mean Square	F	Sig.
PRETEST	Between Groups	240.667	2	120.333	1.600	.229
	Within Groups	1354.000	18	75.222		
	Total	1594.667	20			

The ANOVA was not significant, so there is no need to refer to the Multiple Comparisons table. Given this result, we may state the following:

The pretest means of students who took a course from three different instructors were compared using a one-way ANOVA. No significant difference was found ($F(2,18) = 1.60$, $p > .05$). The students from the three different classes did not differ significantly at the start of the term.

66

Practice Exercise

Using Practice Data Set 1 in Appendix B, determine if the average math scores of single, married, and divorced subjects are significantly different. Write a statement of results.

Section 6.6   Factorial ANOVA

Description

The factorial ANOVA is one in which there is more than one **independent variable**. A 2 x 2 ANOVA, for example, has two **independent variables**, each with two **levels**. A 3 x 2 x 2 ANOVA has three **independent variables**. One has three levels, and the other two have two levels. Factorial ANOVA is very powerful because it allows us to assess the effects of each **independent variable**, plus the effects of the **interaction**.

Assumptions

Factorial ANOVA requires all of the assumptions of one-way ANOVA (i.e., the **dependent variable** must be at the interval or ratio levels and normally distributed). In addition, the **independent variables** should be independent of each other.

SPSS Data Format

SPSS requires one variable for the **dependent variable**, and one variable for each **independent variable**. If we have *any* **independent variable** that is represented as multiple variables (e.g., PRETEST and POSTTEST) we must use the repeated measures ANOVA.

Running the Command

This example uses the GRADES.SAV data file from earlier in this chapter. Click *Statistics*, then *General Linear Model*, then *GLM - General Factorial*.

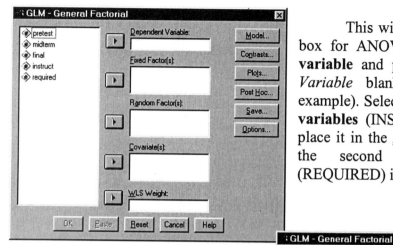

This will bring up the main dialog box for ANOVA. Select the **dependent variable** and place it in the *Dependent Variable* blank (use FINAL for this example). Select one of your **independent variables** (INSTRUCT in this case) and place it in the *Fixed Factor(s)* box. Place the second **independent variable** (REQUIRED) in the *Fixed Factor(s)* box

After you have defined the analysis, click on *Options*. When the options dialog box comes up, move INSTRUCT, REQUIRED, and INSTRUCT x REQUIRED into the *Display Means* blank. This will provide you with means for each main effect and interaction term.

If you select *Post-Hoc*, SPSS will run post-hoc analyses for the main effects, but not for the interaction term.

Reading the Output

At the bottom of the output, you will find the means for each main effect and interaction you selected with the options command.

1. INSTRUCT

Dependent Variable: FINAL

| INSTRUCT | Mean | Std. Error | 95% Confidence Interval | |
			Lower Bound	Upper Bound
1.00	79.583	3.445	72.240	86.926
2.00	86.208	3.445	78.865	93.551
3.00	92.083	3.445	84.740	99.426

There were three instructors, so there is a mean FINAL for each instructor.

We also have means for the two values of REQUIRED.

Finally, we have six means representing the interaction of the two variables (this was a 3 x 2 design).

Subjects who had Instructor 1 and for whom the class was not required had a mean final exam score of 79.67. Students who had Instructor 1 and for whom it was required had a mean final exam score of 79.50, and so on.

2. REQUIRED

Dependent Variable: FINAL

| REQUIRED | Mean | Std. Error | 95% Confidence Interval | |
			Lower Bound	Upper Bound
.00	84.667	3.007	78.257	91.076
1.00	87.250	2.604	81.699	92.801

The sample we just ran is called a two-way *ANOVA*. This is because we had two **independent variables**. With a two-way ANOVA, we get three answers: a main effect for INSTRUCT, a main effect for REQUIRED, and an interaction result for INSTRUCT x REQUIRED.

The source table (at the top of the next page) gives us these three answers. In the example above, none of the main effects or interactions were significant. In the statements of results, you must indicate F, two degrees of freedom (effect and residual), the significance level, and a verbal statement for each of the answers (three in this case).

3. INSTRUCT * REQUIRED

Dependent Variable: FINAL

| INSTRUCT | REQUIRED | Mean | Std. Error | 95% Confidence Interval | |
				Lower Bound	Upper Bound
1.00	.00	79.667	5.208	68.565	90.768
	1.00	79.500	4.511	69.886	89.114
2.00	.00	84.667	5.208	73.565	95.768
	1.00	87.750	4.511	78.136	97.364
3.00	.00	89.667	5.208	78.565	100.768
	1.00	94.500	4.511	84.886	104.114

Tests of Between-Subjects Effects

Dependent Variable: FINAL

Source	Type III Sum of Squares	df	Mean Square	F	Sig.
Corrected Model	635.821[a]	5	127.164	1.563	.230
Intercept	151998.893	1	151998.893	1867.691	.000
INSTRUCT	536.357	2	268.179	3.295	.065
REQUIRED	34.321	1	34.321	.422	.526
INSTRUCT * REQUIRED	22.071	2	11.036	.136	.874
Error	1220.750	15	81.383		
Total	157689.000	21			
Corrected Total	1856.571	20			

a. R Squared = .342 (Adjusted R Squared = .123)

Phrasing Results That Are Significant

If we had obtained significant results in this example, we could state the following (these are fictitious results):

A 3 (instructor) x 2 (required course) between subjects factorial ANOVA was calculated comparing the final exam scores for subjects who had one of three instructors and who took the course as a required course or as an elective. A significant main effect for instructor was found ($F_{(2,15)} = 10.112$, $p < .05$. Students who had Instructor 1 had higher final exam scores ($m = 79.57$, $sd = 7.96$) than students who had Instructor 3 ($m = 92.43$, $sd = 5.50$). Students who had Instructor 2 ($m = 86.43$, $sd = 10.92$) were not significantly different from either of the other two groups. A significant main effect for whether or not the course was required was found ($F_{(1,15)} = 38.44$, $p < .01$). Students who took the course because it was required did better ($m = 91.69$, $sd = 7.68$) than students who took the course as an elective ($m = 77.13$, $sd = 5.72$). The interaction was not significant ($F_{(2,15)} = 1.15$, $p > .05$). The effect of the instructor was not influenced by whether or not the students took the course because it was required.

Note that in the above example, we would have had to conduct Tukey's HSD to determine the differences for INSTRUCTOR (using the Post-Hoc command). This is not necessary for REQUIRED because it has only two levels (and one must be different from the other).

Phrasing Results That Are Not Significant

Our actual results were not significant, so we can state the following:

A 3 (instructor) x 2 (required course) between subjects factorial ANOVA was calculated comparing the final exam scores for subjects who had each instructor and who took the course as a required course or not. The main effect for instructor was not significant ($F(2,15) = 3.30$, $p > .05$). The main effect for whether or not it was a required course was also not significant ($F(1,15) = .42$, $p > .05$). Finally, the interaction was also not significant ($F(2,15) = .136$, $p > .05$). Thus, it appears that neither the instructor nor whether or not the course is required has any significant effect on final exam scores.

Practice Exercise

Using Practice Data Set 2 in Appendix B, determine if salaries are influenced by sex, job classification, or an interaction between sex and job classification. Write a statement of results.

Section 6.7 Repeated Measures ANOVA

Description

Repeated measures ANOVA extends the basic ANOVA procedure to a within-subjects **independent variable** (when subjects provide data for more than one level of an **independent variable**). It functions like a paired samples t test when more than two levels are being compared.

Assumptions

The **dependent variable** should be normally distributed and measured on an interval or ratio scale. Multiple measurements of the **dependent variable** should be from the same (or related) subjects.

SPSS Data Format

At least three variables are required. Each variable in the SPSS data file should represent a single **dependent variable** at a single level of the **independent variable**. Thus, an analysis of a design with four levels of an **independent variable** would require four variables in the SPSS data file.

If any variable represents a between-subjects effect, use the mixed design ANOVA command instead.

Running the Command

This example uses the GRADES.SAV sample data set. Recall that GRADES.SAV includes three sets of grades—PRETEST, MIDTERM, and FINAL—that represent three different times during the semester. This allows us to analyze the effects of time on the test performance of our sample population (hence the within-groups comparison). Click *Statistics*, then *General Linear Model*, then *GLM - Repeated Measures*.

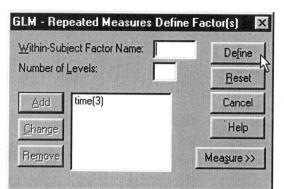

Note that this procedure requires the Advanced Statistics module. If you do not have this command, you do not have the Advanced Statistics module installed.

After selecting the command, you will be presented with the Repeated Measures Define Factors dialog box. This is where you identify the within-subject factor (we'll call it TIME). Enter *3* for the number of levels (three exams), and click *Add*.

Now, click *Define*. If we had more than one **independent variable** that had repeated measures, we could enter its name and click *Add*.

You will be presented with the GLM dialog box. Transfer PRETEST, MIDTERM, and FINAL to the *Within-Subjects Variables* section. The variable names should be ordered according to when they occurred in time (i.e., the values of the **independent variable** that they represent).

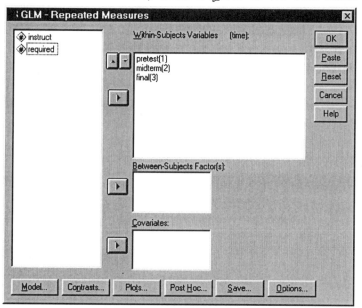

Click *Options*, and SPSS will compute the means for the TIME effect (see one-way ANOVA for more details about how to do this). Click *OK* to run the command.

Reading the Output

This procedure uses the GLM command. GLM stands for "General Linear Model." It is a very powerful command, and many sections of output are beyond the scope of this text (see output outline at right), but for the basic repeated measures ANOVA, we are interested only in the *Tests of Within-Subjects Effects*.

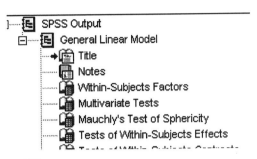

Tests of Within-Subjects Effects

Measure: MEASURE_1

Sphericity Assumed

Source	Type III Sum of Squares	df	Mean Square	F	Sig.	Noncent. Parameter	Observed Power[a]
TIME	5673.746	2	2836.873	121.895	.000	243.791	1.000
Error(TIME)	930.921	40	23.273				

a. Computed using alpha = .05

The *Tests of Within-Subjects Effects* output should look very similar to the output from the other ANOVA commands. In the above example, the effect of TIME has an *F* value of 121.90 with 2 and 40 degrees of freedom. It is significant at less than the .001 level. When describing these results, we should indicate the type of test, *F* value, degrees of freedom, and significance level.

Phrasing Results That Are Significant

Because the ANOVA results were significant, we need to do some sort of post-hoc analysis. One of the main limitations of SPSS is the difficulty in performing post-hoc analyses for within-subjects factors. With SPSS, the easiest solution to this problem is to do **protected dependent *t* tests** with repeated measures ANOVA. There are more powerful (and more appropriate) post-hoc analyses, but SPSS will not compute them for us. For more information, consult a more advanced statistics text or your instructor.

To conduct the protected *t* tests, we will compare PRETEST to MIDTERM, MIDTERM to FINAL, and PRETEST to FINAL, using paired samples *t* tests. Because we are conducting three tests and, therefore, inflating our Type I error rate, we will use a significance level of .017 (.05/3) instead of .05.

Paired Samples Test

| | | Paired Differences | | | | | | | |
| | | Mean | Std. Deviation | Std. Error Mean | 95% Confidence Interval of the Difference | | t | df | Sig. (2-tailed) |
					Lower	Upper			
Pair 1	PRETEST - MIDTERM	-15.2857	3.9641	.8650	-17.0902	-13.4813	-17.670	20	.000
Pair 2	PRETEST - FINAL	-22.8095	8.9756	1.9586	-26.8952	-18.7239	-11.646	20	.000
Pair 3	MIDTERM - FINAL	-7.5238	6.5850	1.4370	-10.5213	-4.5264	-5.236	20	.000

The three comparisons each had a significance level of less than .017, so we can conclude that the scores improved from pretest to midterm and again from midterm to final. To generate the descriptive statistics, we have to run the *Descriptives* command for each variable.

Because the results of our example above were significant, we could state the following:

> A one-way repeated measures ANOVA was calculated comparing the exam scores of subjects at three different times: pretest, midterm, and final. A significant effect was found ($F(2,40) = 121.90$, $p < .001$). Follow-up protected t tests revealed that scores increased significantly from pretest ($m = 63.33$, $sd = 8.93$) to midterm ($m = 78.62$, $sd = 9.66$) and again from midterm to final ($m = 86.14$, $sd = 9.63$).

Phrasing Results That Are Not Significant

With results that are not significant, we could state the following (the F values here have been made up for purposes of illustration):

> A one-way repeated measures ANOVA was calculated comparing the exam scores of subjects at three different times: pretest, midterm, and final. No significant effect was found ($F(2,40) = 1.90$, $p > .05$). No significant difference exists among pretest ($m = 63.33$, $sd = 8.93$), midterm ($m = 78.62$, $sd = 9.66$), and final ($m = 86.14$, $sd = 9.63$) means.

Practice Exercise

Use Practice Data Set 3 in Appendix B. Determine if the anxiety level of subjects changed over time (regardless of which treatment they received). Write a statement of results.

Section 6.8 Mixed-Design ANOVA

Description

The mixed-design ANOVA (sometimes called a split-plot design) tests effects of more than one **independent variable**. At least one of the **independent variables** must be within-subjects (repeated measures). At least one of the **independent variables** must be between-subjects.

Assumptions

The **dependent variable** should be normally distributed and measured on an interval or ratio scale.

SPSS Data Format

The **dependent variable** should be represented as one variable for each level of the within-subjects **independent variables**. Another variable should be present in the data file for each between-subjects variable. Thus, a 2 x 2 mixed design ANOVA would require three variables, two representing the **dependent variable** (one at each level) and one representing the between-subjects **independent variable**.

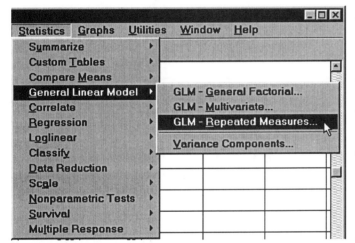

Running the Command

The General Linear Model command runs the mixed-design ANOVA command. Click *Statistics*, then *General Linear Model*, then *GLM Repeated Measures*.

The *GLM - Repeated Measures* command should be used if any of the **independent variables** are repeated measures (within-subjects).

Note that this procedure requires the Advanced Statistics module. If you do not have this command available, you do not have the Advanced Statistics module installed.

This example also uses the GRADES.SAV data file. Enter PRETEST, MIDTERM, and FINAL in the *Within-Subjects Variables* block (see the repeated measures ANOVA command for an explanation). This example is a 3 x 3 mixed design. There are two **independent variables** (TIME and INSTRUCT) each with three levels. We entered the information for TIME in the Repeated Measures Define Factors dialog box.

We need to transfer INSTRUCT into the between-subjects block.

Click *Options* and select means for all of the main effects and the interaction (see one-way ANOVA for more details about how to do this). Click *OK* to run the command.

Reading the Output

As with the standard repeated measures command, the GLM procedure provides a lot of output we will not use. For a mixed design ANOVA, we are interested in two sections. The first is Within-Subjects Effects.

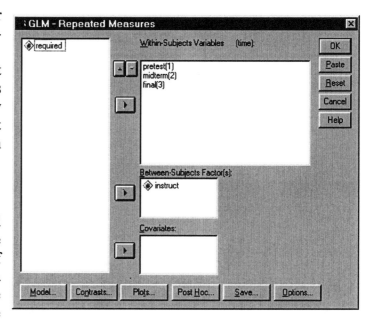

Tests of Within-Subjects Effects

Measure: MEASURE_1

Sphericity Assumed

Source	Type III Sum of Squares	df	Mean Square	F	Sig.	Noncent. Parameter	Observed Power[a]
TIME	5673.746	2	2836.873	817.954	.000	1635.908	1.000
TIME * INSTRUCT	806.063	4	201.516	58.103	.000	232.412	1.000
Error(TIME)	124.857	36	3.468				

a. Computed using alpha = .05

This section gives two of the three answers we need (the main effect for TIME and the interaction result for TIME x INSTRUCTOR). The second section of output is between-subjects (sample output is at the top of the next page). Here, we get the answers that do not contain any within-subjects effects. For our example, we get the main effect for INSTRUCT. Both of these sections must be combined to arrive at the full answer for our analysis.

If we obtain significant effects, we must perform some sort of post-hoc analysis. Again, this is one of the limitations of SPSS. No easy way to perform the appropriate post-hoc test for repeated measures (within-subjects) factors is available. Ask your instructor for assistance with this.

Tests of Between-Subjects Effects

Measure: MEASURE_1

Transformed Variable: Average

Source	Type III Sum of Squares	df	Mean Square	F	Sig.	Noncent. Parameter	Observed Power[a]
Intercept	364192.1	1	364192.1	1500.595	.000	1500.595	1.000
INSTRUCT	18.698	2	9.349	.039	.962	.077	.055
Error	4368.571	18	242.698				

a. Computed using alpha = .05

When describing the results, you should include F, the degrees of freedom, and the significance level for each main effect and interaction. In addition, some descriptive statistics must be included (either give means or include a figure).

Phrasing Results That Are Significant

There are three answers (at least) for all mixed-design ANOVAs. Please see the section on factorial ANOVA for more details about how to interpret and phrase the results. For the above example, we could state the following in the results section (note that this assumes that appropriate post-hoc tests have been conducted):

A 3 x 3 mixed design ANOVA was calculated to examine the effects of the instructor (Instructor 1, 2, and 3) and time (pretest, midterm, final) on scores. A significant time x instructor interaction was present ($F(4,36) = 58.10$, $p <$ .001). In addition, the main effect for time was significant ($F(2,36) = 817.95$, $p < .001$). The main effect for instructor was not significant ($F(2,18) = .039$, p > .05). Upon examination of the data, it appears that Instructor 3 showed the most improvement in scores over time.

With significant interactions, it is often helpful to provide a graph with the descriptive statistics. The graph to the left was computed using the procedures discussed in Chapter 4 (bar charts).

Interactions add considerable complexity to the interpretation of statistical results. Consult a research methods text or your instructor for more help with interactions.

Phrasing Results That Are Not Significant

If our results had not been significant, we could state the following (note that the F values are fictitious):

A 3 x 3 mixed design ANOVA was calculated to examine the effects of instructor (Instructor 1, 2, and 3) and time (pretest, midterm, final) on scores. No significant main effects or interactions were found. The time x instructor interaction ($F(4,36) = 1.10$, $p > .05$), the main effect for time ($F(2,36) = 1.95$, $p > .05$), and the main effect for instructor ($F(2,18) = .039$, $p > .05$) were all not significant. Exam scores were not influenced by either time or instructor.

Practice Exercise

Use Practice Data Set 3 in Appendix B. Determine if anxiety levels changed over time for each of the treatment types. How did time change anxiety levels for each treatment? Write a statement of results.

Section 6.9   Analysis of Covariance

Description

Analysis of Covariance (ANCOVA) allows you to remove the effect of a known **covariate**. In this way, it becomes a statistical method of control. With methodological controls (e.g., random assignment), internal validity is gained. When such methodological controls are not possible, statistical controls can be used.

ANCOVA can be performed by using the GLM command if you have repeated measures factors. Because the GLM command is not included in the Base Statistics module, it is not included here.

Assumptions

ANCOVA requires that the covariate be significantly correlated with the **dependent variable**. The **dependent variable** and the covariate should be at the interval or ratio levels. In addition, both should be normally distributed.

SPSS Data Format

The SPSS data file must contain one variable for each **independent variable**, one variable representing the **dependent variable**, and at least one covariate.

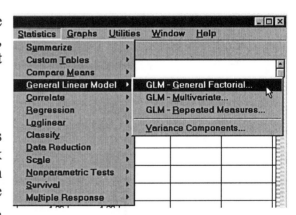

Running the Command

The factorial ANOVA command is used to run ANCOVA. To run it, click *Statistics*, then *General Linear Model*, then *GLM - General Factorial*. Follow the directions discussed for factorial ANOVA, using the HEIGHT.SAV sample data file. Place the variable HEIGHT as your **dependent variable** (see next page). Enter SEX as your fixed factor. Then, enter WEIGHT as the covariate. This last step makes the difference between regular factorial ANOVA and ANCOVA. Click *OK* to run the ANCOVA.

Reading the Output

The output consists of one main source table (shown below). This table gives you the main effects and interactions you would have received with a normal factorial ANOVA. In addition, there is a row for each covariate. In our example, we have one main effect (SEX) and one covariate (WEIGHT). Normally, we examine the covariate line only to confirm that the covariate is significantly related to the **dependent variable**.

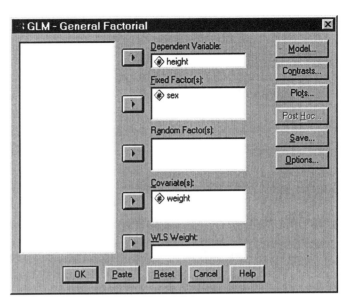

Tests of Between-Subjects Effects

Dependent Variable: HEIGHT

Source	Type III Sum of Squares	df	Mean Square	F	Sig.
Corrected Model	215.027[a]	2	107.513	100.476	.000
Intercept	5.580	1	5.580	5.215	.040
WEIGHT	119.964	1	119.964	112.112	.000
SEX	66.367	1	66.367	62.023	.000
Error	13.911	13	1.070		
Total	71919.000	16			
Corrected Total	228.938	15			

a. R Squared = .939 (Adjusted R Squared = .930)

Drawing Conclusions

This sample analysis was performed to determine if males and females differ in height, after accounting for weight. We know that weight is related to height. Rather than match subjects or use methodological controls, we can statistically remove the effect of weight.

When giving the results of ANCOVA, we must give F, degrees of freedom, and significance levels for all main effects, interactions, and covariates. If main effects or interactions are significant, post-hoc tests must be conducted. Descriptive statistics (mean and standard deviation) for each level of the **independent variable** should also be given.

Phrasing Results That Are Significant

The above example obtained a significant result, so we could state the following:

A one-way between-subjects ANCOVA was calculated to examine the effect of sex on height, covarying out the effect of weight. Weight was significantly related to height ($F(1,13) = 112.11$, $p < .001$). The main effect for sex was significant ($F(1,13) = 62.02$, $p < .001$), with males significantly taller ($m = 69.38$, $sd = 3.70$) than females ($m = 64.50$, $sd = 2.33$).

Phrasing Results That Are Not Significant

If the covariate is not significant, we need to repeat the analysis without including the covariate (i.e., run a normal ANOVA). For results that are not significant, you could state the following (note that the *F* values are made up for this example):

> A one-way between-subjects ANCOVA was calculated to examine the effect of sex on height, covarying out the effect of weight. Weight was significantly related to height ($F(1,13) = 112.11$, $p < .001$). The main effect for sex was not significant ($F(1,13) = 2.02$, $p > .05$), with males not being significantly taller ($m = 69.38$, $sd = 3.70$) than females ($m = 64.50$, $sd = 2.33$), even after covarying out the effect of weight.

Practice Exercise

Using Practice Data Set 2 in Appendix B, determine if salaries are different for males and females. Repeat the analysis, statistically controlling for years of service. Write a statement of results for each. Compare and contrast your two answers.

Section 6.10   Multivariate Analysis of Variance (MANOVA)

Description

Multivariate tests are those that involve more than one **dependent variable**. While it is possible to conduct several univariate tests (one for each **dependent variable**), this causes Type I error inflation. Multivariate tests look at all **dependent variables** at once, in much the same way that ANOVA looks at all levels of an **independent variable** at once.

Assumptions

MANOVA assumes that you have multiple **dependent variables** that are related to each other. Each **dependent variable** should be normally distributed and measured on an interval or ratio scale.

SPSS Data Format

The SPSS data file should have a variable for each **dependent variable**. One additional variable is required for each between-subjects **independent variable**. It is possible to do a repeated-measures MANOVA as well as a MANCOVA and a repeated-measures MANCOVA. These extensions require additional variables in the data file.

Running the Command

The following data represent SAT and GRE scores for 18 subjects. Six subjects received no special training, six received short-term training before taking the tests, and six received long-term training. GROUP is coded $0 =$ no training, $1 =$ short term, $2 =$ long term. Enter the data, and save it as SAT.SAV

SAT	GRE	GROUP
580	600	0
520	520	0
500	510	0
410	400	0
650	630	0
480	480	0
500	490	1
640	650	1
500	480	1
500	510	1
580	570	1
490	500	1
520	520	2
620	630	2
550	560	2
500	510	2
540	560	2
600	600	2

The multivariate command is located by clicking *Statistics*, then *General Linear Model*, then *GLM - Multivariate*. Note that this command requires the Advanced Statistics module.

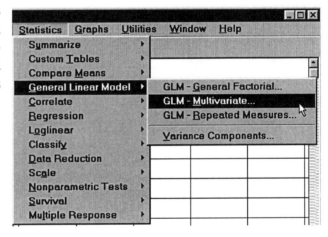

This will bring up the main dialog box. Enter the **dependent variables** (GRE and SAT, in this case) in the Dependent Variables blank. Enter the **independent variable(s)** in the Fixed Factors blank. Click *OK* to run the command.

Reading the Output

We are interested in two primary sections of output. The first one gives the results of the multivariate tests. The section labeled GROUP is the one we want. This tells us whether GROUP had an effect on any of our **dependent variables**. Four different types of Multivariate test results are given. The most widely used is Wilks' Lambda. Thus, the answer for the MANOVA is a Lambda of .828, with 4 and 28 degrees of freedom. That value is not significant.

Multivariate Tests[d]

Effect		Value	F	Hypothesis df	Error df	Sig.	Noncent. Parameter	Observed Power[a]
Intercept	Pillai's Trace	.988	569.187[b]	2.000	14.000	.000	1138.374	1.000
	Wilks' Lambda	.012	569.187[b]	2.000	14.000	.000	1138.374	1.000
	Hotelling's Trace	81.312	569.187[b]	2.000	14.000	.000	1138.374	1.000
	Roy's Largest Root	81.312	569.187[b]	2.000	14.000	.000	1138.374	1.000
GROUP	Pillai's Trace	.174	.713	4.000	30.000	.590	2.852	.203
	Wilks' Lambda	.828	.693[b]	4.000	28.000	.603	2.771	.197
	Hotelling's Trace	.206	.669	4.000	26.000	.619	2.675	.189
	Roy's Largest Root	.196	1.469[c]	2.000	15.000	.261	2.938	.265

a. Computed using alpha = .05

b. Exact statistic

c. The statistic is an upper bound on F that yields a lower bound on the significance level.

d. Design: Intercept+GROUP

The second section of output we want gives the results of the univariate tests (ANOVAs) for each **dependent variable**.

Tests of Between-Subjects Effects

Source	Dependent Variable	Type III Sum of Squares	df	Mean Square	F	Sig.	Noncent. Parameter	Observed Power[a]
Corrected Model	GRE	5200.000[b]	2	2600.000	.587	.568	1.175	.130
	SAT	3077.778[c]	2	1538.889	.360	.703	.721	.097
Intercept	GRE	5248800	1	5248800	1185.723	.000	1185.723	1.000
	SAT	5205689	1	5205689	1219.448	.000	1219.448	1.000
GROUP	GRE	5200.000	2	2600.000	.587	.568	1.175	.130
	SAT	3077.778	2	1538.889	.360	.703	.721	.097
Error	GRE	66400.000	15	4426.667				
	SAT	64033.333	15	4268.889				
Total	GRE	5320400	18					
	SAT	5272800	18					
Corrected Total	GRE	71600.000	17					
	SAT	67111.111	17					

a. Computed using alpha = .05

b. R Squared = .073 (Adjusted R Squared = -.051)

c. R Squared = .046 (Adjusted R Squared = -.081)

Drawing Conclusions

We interpret the results of the univariate tests only if Lambda is significant. Our results are not significant, but we will first consider how to interpret results that are significant.

Phrasing Results That Are Significant

If we had received the following output instead, we would have had a significant MANOVA, and we could state the following (next page):

Multivariate Tests[d]

Effect		Value	F	Hypothesis df	Error df	Sig.	Noncent. Parameter	Observed Power[a]
Intercept	Pillai's Trace	.989	628.447[b]	2.000	14.000	.000	1256.894	1.000
	Wilks' Lambda	.011	628.447[b]	2.000	14.000	.000	1256.894	1.000
	Hotelling's Trace	89.778	628.447[b]	2.000	14.000	.000	1256.894	1.000
	Roy's Largest Root	89.778	628.447[b]	2.000	14.000	.000	1256.894	1.000
GROUP	Pillai's Trace	.967	7.018	4.000	30.000	.000	28.070	.986
	Wilks' Lambda	.047	25.218[b]	4.000	28.000	.000	100.870	1.000
	Hotelling's Trace	19.887	64.633	4.000	26.000	.000	258.531	1.000
	Roy's Largest Root	19.872	149.041[c]	2.000	15.000	.000	298.082	1.000

a. Computed using alpha = .05

b. Exact statistic

c. The statistic is an upper bound on F that yields a lower bound on the significance level.

d. Design: Intercept+GROUP

Tests of Between-Subjects Effects

Source	Dependent Variable	Type III Sum of Squares	df	Mean Square	F	Sig.	Noncent. Parameter	Observed Power[a]
Corrected Model	SAT	3077.778[b]	2	1538.889	.360	.703	.721	.097
	GRE	65200.000[c]	2	32600.000	7.364	.006	14.729	.882
Intercept	SAT	5205689	1	5205689	1219.448	.000	1219.448	1.000
	GRE	4620800	1	4620800	1043.855	.000	1043.855	1.000
GROUP	SAT	3077.778	2	1538.889	.360	.703	.721	.097
	GRE	65200.000	2	32600.000	7.364	.006	14.729	.882
Error	SAT	64033.333	15	4268.889				
	GRE	66400.000	15	4426.667				
Total	SAT	5272800	18					
	GRE	4752400	18					
Corrected Total	SAT	67111.111	17					
	GRE	131600.0	17					

a. Computed using alpha = .05

b. R Squared = .046 (Adjusted R Squared = -.081)

c. R Squared = .495 (Adjusted R Squared = .428)

A one-way MANOVA was calculated examining the effect of training (none, short-term, long-term) on SAT and GRE scores. A significant effect was found (*Lambda*(4,28) = 25.22, $p < .01$). Follow-up univariate ANOVAs indicated that SAT scores were not significantly influenced by training ($F(2,15) = .36$, $p > .05$). GRE scores, however, were significantly improved by training ($F(2,15) = 7.36$, $p < .01$).

Phrasing Results That Are Not Significant

The example presented in the example was not significant. Therefore, we could state the following in the results section:

A one-way MANOVA was calculated examining the effect of training (none, short-term, or long-term) on SAT and GRE scores. No significant effect was found (*Lambda*(4,28) = .828, $p > .05$). Neither SAT nor GRE scores were significantly influenced by training.

Chapter 7

Nonparametric Inferential Statistics

Nonparametric tests are used when the corresponding parametric procedure is inappropriate. Normally this is because the dependent variable is not interval or ratio scaled. It can also be because the dependent variable is not normally distributed. If the data of interest are frequency counts, nonparametric statistics may also be appropriate.

Section 7.1 Chi Square Goodness of Fit

Description

The chi square goodness of fit test determines whether or not sample proportions match the theoretical values. For example, it could be used to determine if a die is "loaded" or fair. It could also be used to compare the proportion of children born with birth defects to the population value (e.g., to determine if a certain neighborhood has a statistically higher than normal rate of birth defects).

Assumptions

We need to make very few assumptions. There are no assumptions about the shape of the distribution. The expected frequencies for each category should be at least 1, and no more than 20% of the categories should have expected frequencies of less than 5.

SPSS Data Format

SPSS requires only a single variable.

Running the Command

We will create the following data set and call it COINS.SAV. The following data represent flipping each of two coins 20 times (H is coded as heads, T as tails).

Coin 1: H T H H T H H T H H H T T T H T H T T H
Coin 2: T T H H T H T H T T H H T H H T H T H H

Name the two variables COIN1 and COIN2, and code H as 1 and T as 2.

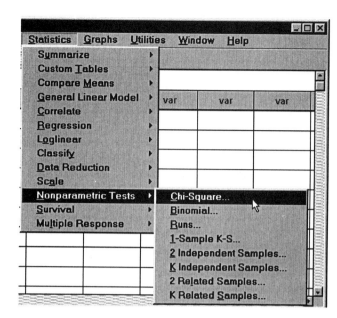

To run the Chi-Square command, click *Statistics*, then *Nonparametric Tests*, then *Chi-Square*. This will bring up the main dialog box for the Chi-Square command.

Transfer the variable COIN1 into the *Test Variable List*. A "fair" coin has an equal chance of coming up heads or tails. Therefore, we will leave the *Expected Values* set to *All categories equal*.

We could test a specific set of proportions by entering the relative frequencies in the *Expected Values* area. Click *OK* to run the analysis.

Reading the Output

COIN1

	Observed N	Expected N	Residual
Head	11	10.0	1.0
Tail	9	10.0	-1.0
Total	20		

The output consists of two sections. The first section gives the frequencies of each value of the variable. The expected value is given, along with the difference from the expected value (called the residual). In our example, with 20 flips of a coin, we should get 10 of each value.

The second section of the output gives the results of the chi-square test.

Test Statistics

	COIN1
Chi-Square[a]	.200
df	1
Asymp. Sig.	.655

a. 0 cells (.0%) have expected frequencies less than 5. The minimum expected cell frequency is 10.0.

Drawing Conclusions

A significant chi-square test indicates that the data vary from the expected values. A test that is not significant indicates that the data are consistent with the expected values.

Phrasing Results That Are Significant

In describing the results, you should state the value of chi square, the degrees of freedom, the significance level, and a description of the results. For example, with a significant chi square (for a sample different from our example above), we could state the following:

A chi square goodness of fit test was calculated comparing the frequency of occurrence of each value of a die. It was hypothesized that each value would occur an equal number of times. A significant deviation from the hypothesized values was found (chi-square(5) = 25.48, $p < .05$).

Note that this example uses hypothetical values.

Phrasing Results That Are Not Significant

If the analysis results in no significant difference, as in the example above, we could state the following:

A chi square goodness of fit test was calculated comparing the frequency of occurrence of heads and tails on a coin. It was hypothesized that each value would occur an equal number of times. No significant deviation from the hypothesized values was found (chi-square(1) = .20, $p > .05$). The coin appears to be fair.

Practice Exercise

Use Practice Data Set 2 in Appendix B. In the entire population from which the sample was drawn, 20% of employees are clerical, 50% are technical, and 30% are professional. Determine whether or not the sample drawn conforms to these values.

Section 7.2   Chi-Square Test of Independence

Description

The chi-square test of independence tests whether or not two variables are independent of each other. For example, flips of a coin should be independent events, so knowing the outcome of one coin toss should not tell us anything about the second coin toss. The chi-square test of independence is essentially a nonparametric version of the interaction term in ANOVA.

Assumptions

There are very few assumptions needed. For example, we make no assumptions about the shape of the distribution. The expected frequencies for each category should be at least 1, and no more than 20% of the categories should have expected frequencies of less than 5.

SPSS Data Format

At least two variables are required.

Running the Command

The chi-square test of independence is a component of the *Crosstabs* command. See the section on frequency distributions for more than one variable in Chapter 3 for more details.

This example uses the COINS.SAV example. COIN1 is placed in the rows blank and COIN2 is placed in the Columns blank.

Click *Statistics* and then check the *Chi-square* box. Click *Continue.* You may also want to click *Cells* to select expected frequencies.

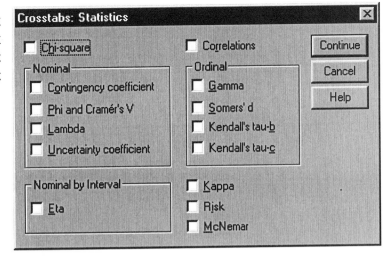

COIN1 * COIN2 Crosstabulation

| | | | COIN2 | | |
			Head	Tail	Total
COIN1	Head	Count	7	4	11
		Expected Count	6.1	5.0	11.0
	Tail	Count	4	5	9
		Expected Count	5.0	4.1	9.0
Total		Count	11	9	20
		Expected Count	11.0	9.0	20.0

Reading the Output

The output consists of two parts. The first part gives you the counts. In this example, the actual and expected frequencies are shown because they were selected using the *Cells* option.

The second part of the output gives the results of the chi-square test. The most commonly used value is the Pearson chi-square, shown in the first row (value of .737).

Chi-Square Tests

	Value	df	Asymp. Sig. (2-sided)	Exact Sig. (2-sided)	Exact Sig. (1-sided)
Pearson Chi-Square	.737[b]	1	.391		
Continuity Correction[a]	.165	1	.684		
Likelihood Ratio	.740	1	.390		
Fisher's Exact Test				.653	.342
Linear-by-Linear Association	.700	1	.403		
N of Valid Cases	20				

a. Computed only for a 2x2 table

b. 3 cells (75.0%) have expected count less than 5. The minimum expected count is 4.05.

Drawing Conclusions

A significant chi-square test result indicates that the two variables are not independent. A value that is not significant indicates that the variables do not vary significantly from independence.

Phrasing Results That Are Significant

In describing the results, you should give the value of chi-square, the degrees of freedom, the significance level, and a description of the results. For example, with a significant chi-square (for a data set different from the one discussed above), we could state the following:

> A chi-square test of independence was calculated comparing the frequency of heart disease for men and women. A significant interaction was found (chi square(1) = 23.80, $p < .05$). Men were more likely to get heart disease (68%) than women (40%).

Note that this summary statement assumes that a test was run in which subjects' sex as well as whether or not they had heart disease were coded.

Phrasing Results That Are Not Significant

A chi-square that is not significant indicates that there is no significant dependence of one variable on the other. The coin example above was not significant. Therefore, we could state the following:

> A chi square test of independence was calculated comparing the result of flipping two coins. No significant relationship was found (chi-square(1) = .737, $p > .05$). Flips of a coin appear to be independent events.

Practice Exercise

A researcher is interested in knowing whether or not people are more likely to help in an emergency when they are indoors or outdoors. Of 28 subjects who were outdoors, 19 helped and 9 did not. Of 23 subjects who were indoors, 8 helped and 15 did not. Enter these data, and find out if helping behavior is affected by the environment. The trick to this problem is in the data entry. (Hint: How many subjects were there, and what do you know about each subject?)

Section 7.3 Mann-Whitney U Test

Description

The Mann-Whitney U test is the nonparametric equivalent of the independent t test. It tests whether or not two independent samples are from the same distribution. The Mann-Whitney U is weaker than the independent t test, and the t test should be used if you can meet its assumptions.

Assumptions

The Mann-Whitney U test uses the rankings of the data. Therefore, the data for the two samples must be at least ordinal. There are no assumptions about the shape of the distribution.

SPSS Data Format

This command requires a single variable representing the **dependent variable** and a second variable indicating group membership.

	long	medium	short	experien
1	1	4	6	2
2	2	3	4	2
3	3	2	7	2
4	4	5	3	2
5	5	1	10	1
6	6	8	5	1
7	7	7	12	1
8	8	6	1	1
9	9	10	3	0
10	10	9	9	0
11	11	11	11	0
12	12	12	2	0

Running the Command

This example will use a new data file. It represents 12 subjects in a series of races. There were long races, medium races, and short races. Subjects either had a lot of experience (2), some experience (1), or no experience (0).

Enter the data from the figure to the left in a new file, and save the data file as RACE.SAV. The values for LONG, MEDIUM, and SHORT represent the results of the race, with 1 being first place and 12 being last.

To run the command, click *Statistics*, then *Nonparametric Tests*, then *2 Independent Samples*. That will bring up the main dialog box.

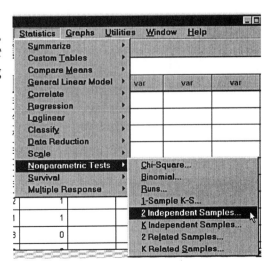

Enter the dependent variable (LONG for this example) in the *Test Variable List* blank. Enter the Independent Variable (EXPERIEN) as the *Grouping Variable*. Make sure that *Mann-Whitney U* is checked.

Click *Define Groups* to select which two groups you will compare. For this example, let's compare those runners with no experience (0) to those runners with a lot of experience (2).

Reading the Output

The output consists of two sections. The first section gives descriptive statistics for the two samples. Because the data are only required to be ordinal, summaries relating to their ranks are used. Those subjects who had no experience averaged 6.5 as their place in the race. Those subjects with a lot of experience averaged 2.5 as their place in the race.

Ranks

	EXPERIEN	N	Mean Rank	Sum of Ranks
LONG	0	4	6.50	26.00
	2	4	2.50	10.00
	Total	8		

Test Statistics[b]

	LONG
Mann-Whitney U	.000
Wilcoxon W	10.000
Z	-2.309
Asymp. Sig. (2-tailed)	.021
Exact Sig. [2*(1-tailed Sig.)]	.029[a]

a. Not corrected for ties.

b. Grouping Variable: EXPERIEN

The second section of the output is the result of the Mann-Whitney *U* test itself. The value obtained was 0.0, with a significance level of .021.

Drawing Conclusions

A significant Mann-Whitney U result indicates that the two samples are different.

Phrasing Results That Are Significant

Our example above is significant, so we could state the following:

A Mann-Whitney U test was calculated examining the place that runners with varying levels of experience took in a long-distance race. Runners with no experience did significantly worse (m place = 6.5) than runners with a lot of experience (m place = 2.5; $U = 0, p < .05$).

Phrasing Results That Are Not Significant

If we conduct the analysis on the short-distance race instead of the long-distance race, we will get the following results, which are not significant.

Ranks

	EXPERIEN	N	Mean Rank	Sum of Ranks
SHORT	0	4	4.63	18.50
	2	4	4.38	17.50
	Total	8		

Test Statistics[b]

	SHORT
Mann-Whitney U	7.500
Wilcoxon W	17.500
Z	-.145
Asymp. Sig. (2-tailed)	.885
Exact Sig. [2*(1-tailed Sig.)]	.886[a]

a. Not corrected for ties.

b. Grouping Variable: EXPERIEN

Therefore, we could state the following:

A Mann-Whitney U test was used to examine the difference in the race performance of runners with no experience and runners with a lot of experience in a short-distance race. No significant difference in the results of the race was found ($U = 7.50, p > .05$). Runners with no experience averaged a place of 4.63. Runners with a lot of experience averaged 4.38.

Practice Exercise

Assume that the mathematics scores in Practice Exercise 1 (Appendix B) are measured on an ordinal scale. Determine if younger subjects (< 25) have significantly lower mathematics scores than older subjects.

Section 7.4 Wilcoxon Test

Description

The Wilcoxon test is the nonparametric equivalent of the paired samples (dependent) *t* test. It tests whether or not two related samples are from the same distribution. The Wilcoxon test is weaker than the independent *t* test, so the *t* test should be used if you can meet its assumptions.

Assumptions

The Wilcoxon test is based on the difference in rankings. The data for the two samples must be at least ordinal. There are no assumptions about the shape of the distribution.

SPSS Data Format

The test requires two variables. One variable represents the dependent variable at one level of the independent variable. The other variable represents the dependent variable at the second level of the independent variable.

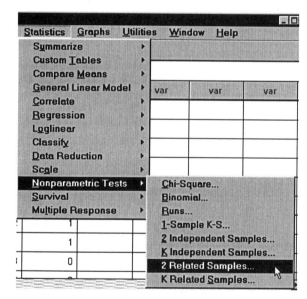

Running the Command

The command is located by clicking *Statistics*, then *Nonparametric Tests*, then *2 Related Samples*. This example uses the RACE.SAV data set.

This will bring up the dialog box for the Wilcoxon test. Note the similarity between it and the dialog box for the dependent *t* test. If you have trouble, refer to the section on the dependent (paired samples) *t* test in Chapter 6.

Transfer the variables LONG and MEDIUM as a pair and run the test. This will determine if the runners perform equivalently on long- and medium-distance races.

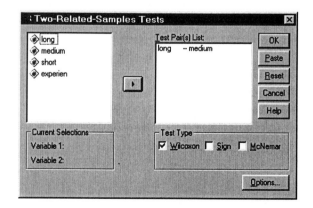

Reading the Output

The output consists of two parts. The first part gives summary statistics for the two variables. The second section contains the result of the Wilcoxon test (given as Z).

Ranks

		N	Mean Rank	Sum of Ranks
MEDIUM - LONG	Negative Ranks	4[a]	5.38	21.50
	Positive Ranks	5[b]	4.70	23.50
	Ties	3[c]		
	Total	12		

a. MEDIUM < LONG

b. MEDIUM > LONG

c. LONG = MEDIUM

Test Statistics[b]

	MEDIUM - LONG
Z	-.121[a]
Asymp. Sig. (2-tailed)	.904

a. Based on negative ranks.

b. Wilcoxon Signed Ranks Test

The example here shows that no significant difference was found between the results of the long-distance and medium-distance races.

Phrasing Results That Are Significant

A significant result means that a change has occurred between the two measurements. If that happened, we could state the following:

A Wilcoxon test examined the results of the short- and long-distance races. A significant difference was found in the results ($Z = 3.40$, $p < .05$). Short-distance results were better than long-distance results.

Note that these results are fictitious.

Phrasing Results That Are Not Significant

In fact, the results in the example above were not significant, so we could state the following:

A Wilcoxon test examined the results of the medium and long-distance races. No significant difference was found in the results ($Z = -121$, $p > .05$). Medium-distance results were not significantly different from long-distance results.

Practice Exercise

Use the RACE.SAV data file to determine whether or not the outcome of short-distance races is different from medium-distance races. Phrase your results.

Section 7.5   Kruskal-Wallis *H* Test

Description

The Kruskal-Wallis *H* test is the nonparametric equivalent of the one-way ANOVA. It tests whether or not several independent samples come from the same population.

Assumptions

Because it is a nonparametric test, there are very few assumptions. However, the test does assume an ordinal level of measurement.

SPSS Data Format

SPSS requires one variable to represent the dependent variable and another to represent the levels of the independent variable.

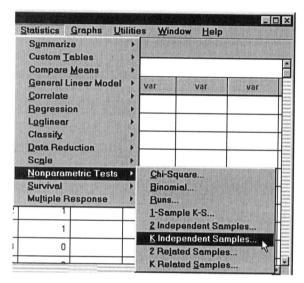

Running the Command

This example uses the RACE.SAV data file. To run the command, click *Statistics*, then *Nonparametric Tests*, then *K independent samples*. This will bring up the main dialog box.

Enter the independent variable as the *Grouping Variable* (EXPERIEN), and click *Define Range* to define the lowest (0) and highest (2) values. Enter the dependent variable in the *Test Variable List*, and click *OK*.

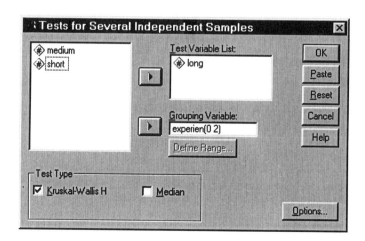

96

Ranks

EXPERIEN		N	Mean Rank
LONG	0	4	10.50
	1	4	6.50
	2	4	2.50
	Total	12	

Reading the Output

The output consists of two parts. The first part gives summary statistics for each of the groups defined by the grouping (independent) variable.

The second part of the output gives the results of the Kruskal-Wallis test (given as a chi-square value, but we will describe it as an *H*). The example here is a significant value of 9.846.

Drawing Conclusions

Like the one-way ANOVA, the Kruskal-Wallis test assumes that the groups are equal. Thus, a significant result indicates that at least one of the groups is different from at least one other group. Unlike the one-way ANOVA command, however, there are no options available for post-hoc analysis.

Test Statistics[a,b]

	LONG
Chi-Square	9.846
df	2
Asymp. Sig.	.007

a. Kruskal Wallis Test

b. Grouping Variable: EXPERIEN

Phrasing Results That Are Significant

The example above is significant, so we could state the following:

A Kruskal-Wallis test was conducted comparing the outcome of a long-distance race for runners with varying levels of experience. A significant result was found ($H(2) = 9.85$, $p < .01$) indicating that the groups differed from each other. Runners with no experience averaged a placement of 10.5, while runners with some experience averaged 6.5 and runners with a lot of experience averaged 2.5. The more experience the runners had, the better they did.

Phrasing Results That Are Not Significant

If we conducted the analysis using the results of the short-distance race, we would get the following output, which is not significant.

Ranks

EXPERIEN		N	Mean Rank
SHORT	0	4	6.38
	1	4	7.25
	2	4	5.88
	Total	12	

Test Statistics[a,b]

	SHORT
Chi-Square	.299
df	2
Asymp. Sig.	.861

a. Kruskal Wallis Test

b. Grouping Variable: EXPERIEN

This result is not significant, so we could state the following:

A Kruskal-Wallis test was conducted comparing the outcome of a short distance race for runners with varying levels of experience. No significant difference was found ($H(2) = .299, p > .05$), indicating that the groups did not differ significantly from each other. Runners with no experience averaged a placement of 6.38, while runners with some experience averaged 7.25 and runners with a lot of experience averaged 5.88. Experience did not seem to influence the results of the short-distance race.

Practice Exercise

Use Practice Data Set 2 in Appendix B. Job classification is ordinal (clerical < technical < professional). Determine if males and females have different levels of job classification. Phrase your results.

Section 7.6   Friedman Test

Description

The Friedman test is the nonparametric equivalent of a one-way repeated measures ANOVA. It is used when you have more than two measurements from related subjects.

Assumptions

The test uses the rankings of the variables, so the data must be at least ordinal. No other assumptions are required.

SPSS Data Format

SPSS requires at least three variables in the SPSS data file. Each variable represents the dependent variable at one of the levels of the independent variable.

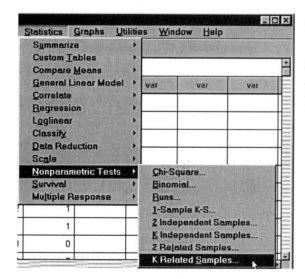

Running the Command

The command is located by clicking *Statistics*, then *Nonparametric Tests*, then *K Related Samples*. This will bring up the main dialog box.

Place all of the variables representing the levels of the independent variable in the *Test Variables* area. For this example, use the RACE.SAV data file and the variables LONG, MEDIUM, and SHORT.

Reading the Output

The output consists of two sections. The first section gives you summary statistics for each of the variables. The second part of the output gives you the results of the test as a chi-square value. The example here has a value of .049 and is not significant (Asymp. Sig., otherwise known as *p*, is .976, which is greater than .05).

Ranks

	Mean Rank
LONG	2.00
MEDIUM	2.04
SHORT	1.96

Drawing Conclusions

The Friedman test assumes that the three variables are from the same population. A significant value indicates that the variables are not equivalent.

Test Statistics[a]

N	12
Chi-Square	.049
df	2
Asymp. Sig.	.976

a. Friedman Test

Phrasing Results That Are Significant

If we obtained a significant result, we could state the following (these are hypothetical results):

A Friedman test was conduced comparing the average class ranking of students in grade school, high school, and college. A significant difference was found (chi square(2) = 34.12, *p* < .05). Students did better in grade school than in high school, and better in high school than in college.

Phrasing Results That Are Not Significant

In fact, the example above was not significant, so we could state the following:

A Friedman test was conducted comparing the average place in a race of runners for short-range, medium-range, and long-range races. No significant difference was found (chi-square(2) = .049, *p* > .05). The length of race did not significantly impact the results of the race.

Practice Exercise

Use the data in Practice Data Set 3 in Appendix B. If anxiety is measured on an ordinal scale, determine if anxiety levels changed over time. Phrase your results.

Notes

Chapter 8

Test Construction

Section 8.1 Item-Total Analysis

Description

Item-total analysis is a way to assess the **internal consistency** of a data set. As such, it is one of many tests of **reliability**. Item-total analysis comprises a number of items that make up a scale or test that is designed to measure a single construct (e.g., Intelligence), and determines the degree to which all of the items measure the same construct. It does not tell you if it is measuring the correct construct (that is a question of **validity**). Before a test can be valid, however, it must first be reliable.

Assumptions

All the items in the scale should be measured on an interval or ratio scale. In addition, each item should be normally distributed. If your items are ordinal in nature, you can conduct the analysis using the Spearman *rho* correlation instead of the Pearson *r* correlation.

SPSS Data Format

SPSS requires one variable for each item (or question) in the scale. In addition, you must have a variable representing the total score for the scale.

Conducting the Test

Item-total analysis uses the Pearson Correlation command. To conduct it, open the QUESTIONS.SAV data file you created in Chapter 2. Click *Statistics*, then *Correlate*, then *Bivariate*.

Place all questions and the total in the right hand window, and click *OK* (for more help on conducting correlations, see Chapter 5). The total can be calculated using the techniques discussed in Chapter 2.

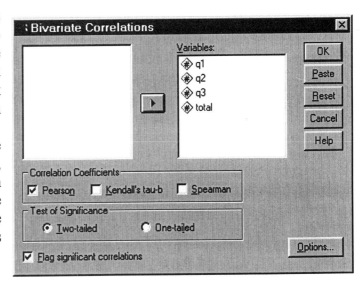

Reading the Output

The output consists of a correlation matrix containing all questions and the total.

Use the column labeled TOTAL, and locate the correlation between the total score and each question. In the example above, Question 1 has a correlation of .873 with the total score. Question 2 has a correlation of −.130 with the total. Question 3 has a correlation of .926 with the total.

Correlations

		Q1	Q2	Q3	TOTAL
Q1	Pearson Correlation	1.000	-.447	.718	.873
	Sig. (2-tailed)	.	.553	.282	.127
	N	4	4	4	4
Q2	Pearson Correlation	-.447	1.000	-.229	-.130
	Sig. (2-tailed)	.553	.	.771	.870
	N	4	4	4	4
Q3	Pearson Correlation	.718	-.229	1.000	.926
	Sig. (2-tailed)	.282	.771	.	.074
	N	4	4	4	4
TOTAL	Pearson Correlation	.873	-.130	.926	1.000
	Sig. (2-tailed)	.127	.870	.074	.
	N	4	4	4	4

Interpreting the Output

Item-total correlations should always be positive. If you obtain a negative correlation, that question should be removed from the scale (or you may consider whether it should be reverse keyed).

Generally, item-total correlations of greater than .7 are considered desirable. Those of less than .3 are considered weak. Any questions with correlations of less than .3 should be removed from the scale.

Normally, the worst question is removed, then the total is recalculated. After the total is recalculated, the item-total analysis is repeated without the question that was removed. Then, if any questions have correlations of less than .3, the worst one is removed, and the process is repeated.

When all remaining correlations are greater than .3, the remaining items in the scale are considered to be the items that are internally consistent.

Section 8.2   Cronbach's Alpha

Description

Cronbach's alpha is a measure of **internal consistency**. As such, it is one of many tests of **reliability**. Cronbach's alpha comprises a number of items that make up a scale designed to measure a single construct (e.g., Intelligence), and determines the degree to which all the items are measuring the same construct. It does not tell you if it is measuring the correct construct (that is a question of **validity**). Before a test can be valid, however, it must first be reliable.

Assumptions

All the items in the scale should be measured on an interval or ratio scale. In addition, each item should be normally distributed.

SPSS Data Format

SPSS requires one variable for each item (or question) in the scale.

Running the Command

This example uses the QUESTIONS.SAV data file we first created in Chapter 2. Click *Statistics*, then *Scale*, then *Reliability Analysis*.

Note that Cronbach's Alpha is part of the *Professional Statistics* module of SPSS. If the *Scale* command does not appear under the *Statistics* menu, you do not have the *Professional Statistics* module installed, and you will not be able to run this command.

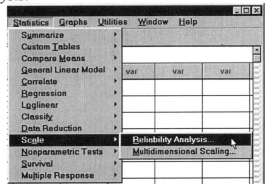

This will bring up the main dialog box for Reliability Analysis. Transfer the questions from your scale to the *Items* blank, and click *OK*.

Note that by changing the options under *Model*, additional measures of internal consistency (e.g., Split-Half) can be calculated.

Reading the Output

In this example, the reliability coefficient is .7365. Numbers close to 1.00 are very good, but numbers close to 0.00 represent poor internal consistency.

Reliability

```
****** Method 1 (space saver) will be used for this analysis ******
▫


    R E L I A B I L I T Y   A N A L Y S I S   -   S C A L E   (A L P H A)


Reliability Coefficients

N of Cases =      10.0              N of Items =   3

Alpha =      .7365
```

Section 8.3   Test-Retest Reliability

Description

Test-retest reliability is a measure of **temporal stability**. As such, it is a measure of reliability. Unlike measures of internal consistency that tell you the extent to which all of the questions that make up a scale measure the same construct, measures of temporal stability tell you whether or not the instrument is consistent over time and/or over multiple administrations.

Assumptions

The total score for the scale should be an interval or ratio scale. The scale scores should be normally distributed.

SPSS Data Format

SPSS requires a variable representing the total score for the scale at the time of first administration. A second variable representing the total score for the same subjects at a different time (normally two weeks later) is also required.

Running the Command

The test-retest reliability coefficient is simply a Pearson correlation coefficient for the relationship between the total scores for the two administrations. To compute the coefficient, follow the directions for computing a Pearson correlation (Section 5.1). Use the two variables representing the two administrations of the test.

Reading the Output

The correlation between the two scores is the test-retest reliability coefficient. It should be positive. Strong reliability is indicated by values close to 1.00. Weak reliability is indicated by values close to 0.00.

Section 8.4   Criterion-Related Validity

Description

Criterion-related validity determines the extent to which the scale you are testing correlates with a criterion. For example, ACT scores should correlate highly with GPA. If they do, that is a measure of validity for ACT scores. If they do not, that indicates that ACT scores may not be valid for the intended purpose.

Assumptions

All of the same assumptions for the Pearson correlation coefficient apply to measures of criterion-related validity (interval or ratio scales, normal distribution, etc.).

SPSS Data Format

Two variables are required. One variable represents the total score for the scale you are testing. The other represents the criterion you are testing it against.

Running the Command

Calculating criterion-related validity involves determining the Pearson correlation value between the scale and the criterion. See Section 5.1 for complete information.

Reading the Output

The correlation between the two scores is the criterion-related validity coefficient. It should be positive. Strong validity is indicated by values close to 1.00. Weak validity is indicated by values close to 0.00.

Appendix A

Determining the Appropriate Significance Test

The following decision tree will help you select the appropriate inferential statistical test. Note that you may be required to compute descriptive statistics in addition to inferential statistics.

1. How many Dependent Variables do you have?
   If one, skip to Step 5.
   If more than one, go to Step 2.
2. Are all your Dependent Variables measured on an interval or ratio scale and normally distributed?
   If yes, go to Step 3.
   If no, skip to Step 4.
3. You need to conduct a MANOVA (Section 6.10).
4. You need a multivariate nonparametric procedure not discussed in this text.
5. Is your Dependent Variable measured on an interval or ratio scale and is it normally distributed?
   If yes, go to Step 6.
   If no, skip to Step 21.
6. How many Independent Variables do you have?
   If none, and you are comparing a single sample to a population, go to Step 7.
   If one, skip to Step 8.
   If more than one, skip to Step 16.
7. You need to conduct a single sample *t*-test (Section 6.2).
8. How many levels does your Independent Variable have?
   If two, go to Step 9.
   If more than two, skip to Step 12.
   If many, and it is measured on a continuous scale, skip to Step 15.
9. Did each subject provide you with data for both levels of the Independent Variable?
   If no, and each subject gave you only one piece of data, go to Step 10.
   If yes, skip to Step 11.
10. You need to conduct an independent samples *t*-test (Section 6.3).
11. You need to conduct a paired samples *t*-test (Section 6.4).

12. Did each subject provide you with data for all levels of the Independent Variable?
    If no, and each subject gave you only one piece of data, go to Step 13.
    If yes, skip to Step 14.
13. You need to conduct a one-way ANOVA (Section 6.5).
14. You need to conduct a repeated-measures ANOVA (Section 6.7).
15. You need to conduct a simple linear regression (Section 5.3).
16. Are your Independent Variables measured on a continuous or dichotomous scale?
    If yes, go to Step 17.
    If no, skip to Step 18.
17. You need to conduct a multiple linear regression (Section 5.4).
18. Did each subject provide you with only one measurement of the Dependent Variable?
    If yes, go to Step 19.
    If no, skip to Step 20.
19. You need to conduct a factorial ANOVA (Section 6.6).
20. You need to conduct a repeated-measures ANOVA (Section 6.7).
21. How many Independent Variables do you have?
    If one, go to Step 22.
    If more than one, skip to Step 29.
22. How many levels does your Independent Variable have?
    If two, go to Step 23.
    If more than two, skip to Step 26.
23. Did each subject give you scores for the Dependent Variable for each level?
    If yes (repeated measures), go to Step 24.
    If no (between subjects), skip to Step 25.
24. You need to conduct a Wilcoxon test (Section 7.4).
25. You need to conduct a Mann-Whitney U procedure (Section 7.3).
26. Did each subject give you scores for the Dependent Variable for each level?
    If yes (repeated measures), go to Step 27.
    If no (between subjects), skip to Step 28.
27. You need to conduct a Friedman test (Section 7.6).
28. You need to conduct a Kruskal-Wallis H test (Section 7.5).
29. Are you interested in relative frequencies of events?
    If yes, go to Step 30.
    If no, skip to Step 31.
30. You need to conduct a chi-square test of independence (Section 7.2).
31. You need to conduct a nonparametric procedure that was not discussed in this text.

Appendix B

Practice Exercise Data Sets

The practice exercises given throughout the text use a variety of data. Some practice exercises use the data sets used in the examples. Others use longer data sets. The longer data sets are presented here.

Practice Data Set 1

You have conducted a study in which you collected data from 20 subjects. You asked each subject to indicate his/her sex (SEX), age (AGE), and marital status (MARITAL). You gave each subject a test to measure mathematics skills (SKILL), where the higher scores indicate a higher skill level. The data are presented below. Note that you will have to code the variables SEX and MARITAL .

SEX	AGE	MARITAL	SKILL
M	23	Single	34
F	35	Married	40
F	40	Divorced	38
M	19	Single	20
M	28	Married	30
F	35	Divorced	40
F	20	Single	38
F	29	Single	47
M	29	Married	26
M	40	Married	24
F	24	Single	45
M	23	Single	37
F	18	Single	44
M	21	Single	38
M	50	Divorced	32
F	25	Single	29
F	20	Single	38
M	24	Single	19
F	37	Married	29
M	42	Married	42
M	35	Married	59
M	23	Single	45
F	40	Divorced	20

Practice Data Set 2

A survey is conducted of employees. Each employee provides the following information: Salary (SALARY), Years of Service (YOS), Sex (SEX), Job Classification (CLASSIFY), and Education Level (EDUC). Note that you will have to code SEX (Male = 1, Female = 2) and CLASSIFY (Clerical = 1, Technical = 2, Professional = 3).

SALARY	YOS	SEX	CLASSIFY	EDUC
35,000	8	Male	Technical	14
18,000	4	Female	Clerical	10
20,000	1	Male	Professional	16
50,000	20	Female	Professional	16
38,000	6	Male	Professional	20
20,000	6	Female	Clerical	12
75,000	17	Male	Professional	20
40,000	4	Female	Technical	12
30,000	8	Male	Technical	14
22,000	15	Female	Clerical	12
23,000	16	Male	Clerical	12
45,000	2	Female	Professional	16

Practice Data Set 3

Subjects who have phobias are given one of three treatments (CONDIT). Their anxiety level (1 to 10) is measured before treatment (ANXPRE), one hour after treatment (ANX1HR), and again four hours after treatment (ANX4HR). Note that you will have to code the variable CONDIT.

ANXPRE	ANX1HR	ANX4HR	CONDIT
8	7	7	Placebo
10	10	10	Placebo
9	7	8	Placebo
7	6	6	Placebo
7	7	7	Placebo
9	4	5	Valium™
10	6	8	Valium™
9	5	5	Valium™
8	3	5	Valium™
6	3	4	Valium™
8	5	3	Experimental Drug
6	5	2	Experimental Drug
9	8	4	Experimental Drug
10	9	4	Experimental Drug
7	6	3	Experimental Drug

Appendix C

Glossary

All Inclusive. A set of events that encompasses every possible outcome.

Alternative Hypothesis. The opposite of the null hypothesis, normally showing that there is a true difference. Generally, this is the statement that the researcher would like to support.

Case Processing Summary. A section of SPSS output that lists the number of subjects used in the analysis.

Coefficient of Determination. The value of the correlation, squared. It provides the proportion of variance accounted for by the relationship.

Continuous. A variable that can have any number of values. No two values exist where there cannot be another value between them (e.g., length).

Correlation Matrix. A section of SPSS output in which correlation coefficients are reported for all pairs of variables.

Covariate. A variable known to be related to the dependent variable, but not treated as an Independent Variable. Used in ANCOVA as a statistical control technique.

Data Window. The SPSS window that contains the data in a spreadsheet format. This is the window used to run most commands.

Dependent Events. When one event gives you information about another event, the events are said to be dependent (e.g., height and weight).

Dependent Variable. An outcome or response variable. The dependent variable is normally dependent on the independent variable.

Descriptive Statistics. Statistical procedures that organize and summarize data.

Dialog Box. A window that allows you to enter information for SPSS to use in a command.

Dichotomous Variables. Variables with only two levels (e.g., gender).

Discrete Variable. A variable that can have only certain values. These are values where there is no score between those values (e.g., A, B, C, D, F).

Frequency Polygon. A graph that represents the frequency of the scores on the Y axis and the scores on the X axis.

Grouping Variable. In SPSS, the variable used to represent group membership. SPSS often refers to independent variables as grouping variables. Sometimes, grouping variables are referred to in SPSS as independent variables.

Independent Events. Two events are independent if information about one event gives you no information about the second event (e.g., two flips of a coin).

Independent Variable. The variable whose levels (values) determine the group to which a subject belongs. A true independent variable is manipulated by the researcher. See grouping variable.

Inferential Statistics. Statistical procedures designed to allow the researcher to draw inferences about a population based on a sample.

Inflated Type I Error Rate. When multiple inferential statistics are computed, the Type I error rate of each compounds and increases the overall probability of making a Type I error.

Interaction. With more than one independent variable, an interaction occurs when a level of one independent variable affects the influence of another independent variable.

Internal Consistency. A reliability measure that assesses the extent to which all of the items in an instrument measure the same construct.

Interval Scale. A measurement scale where items are placed in mutually exclusive categories, with equal intervals between values. Appropriate transformations include counting, sorting, and addition/subtraction.

Levels. The values that a variable can have. A variable with three levels has three possible values.

Mean. A measure of central tendency where the sum of the deviation scores is zero.

Median. A measure of central tendency representing the middle of a distribution when the data are sorted from low to high. Fifty percent of the cases are below the median.

Mode. A measure of central tendency representing the value (or values) with the most subjects (the score with the greatest frequency).

Mutually Exclusive. Two events are mutually exclusive when they can not occur simultaneously.

Nominal Scale. A measurement scale where items are placed in mutually exclusive categories. Differentiation is by name only (e.g., race, sex). Appropriate statements include same or different. Appropriate transformations include counting.

Normal Distribution. A symmetric, unimodal, bell-shaped curve.

Null Hypothesis. The hypothesis to be tested, normally that there is no true difference. It is mutually exclusive of the alternative hypothesis. Also, all inclusive with the null hypothesis.

Ordinal Scale. A measurement scale where items are placed in mutually exclusive categories, in order. Appropriate statements include same, less, and more. Appropriate transformations include counting and sorting.

Outliers. Extreme scores in a distribution. Scores very distant from the mean and the rest of the scores in the distribution.

Output Window. The SPSS window that contains the results of an analysis. The left side summarizes the results in an outline. The right side contains the actual results.

Percentiles (Percentile Ranks). A relative score that gives the percentage of subjects who scored at the same value or lower.

Protected Dependent *t* Tests. To prevent the inflation of a Type I error, the level needed to be significant is reduced when multiple tests are conducted.

Quartiles. The points that define a distribution into four equal parts. The scores at the 25th, 50th, and 75th percentile ranks.

Random Assignment. A procedure for assigning subjects to conditions in which each subject has an equal chance of being assigned to any condition.

Random Selection. A procedure for selecting subjects in which every member of the population has an equal chance of being in the sample.

Range. A measure of dispersion representing the number of points from the highest score through the lowest score.

Ratio Scale. A measurement scale where items are placed in mutually exclusive categories, with equal intervals between values, and a true zero. Appropriate transformations include counting, sorting, addition/subtraction, and multiplication/division.

Reliability. An indication of the consistency of a scale. A reliable scale is internally consistent and stable over time.

Robust. A test is said to be robust if it continues to provide accurate results even after the violation of some assumptions.

Significance. A difference is said to be significant if the probability of making a Type I error is less than the accepted limit (normally 5%). If a difference is significant, the null hypothesis is rejected.

Skew. The extent to which a distribution is not symmetrical. Positive skew has outliers on the right side of the distribution. Negative skew has outliers on the negative (left) side of the distribution.

Standard Deviation. A measure of dispersion representing a special type of average deviation from the mean.

Standard Error of Estimate. The equivalent of the standard deviation for a regression line. The data points will be normally distributed around the regression line with a standard deviation equal to the standard error of the estimate.

Standard Normal Distribution. A normal distribution with a mean of 0 and a standard deviation of 1.

String Variable. A string variable can contain letters and numbers. Numeric variables can contain only numbers. Most SPSS commands will not function with string variables.

Temporal Stability. This is achieved when reliability measures have determined that scores remain stable over multiple administrations of the instrument.

Type I Error. A Type I error occurs when the researcher erroneously rejects the null hypothesis.

Type II Error. A Type II error occurs when the researcher erroneously fails to reject the null hypothesis.

Valid Data. Data that SPSS will use in its analyses.

Validity. An indication of the accuracy of a scale.

Variance. A measure of dispersion equal to the squared standard deviation.

Appendix D

Sample Data Files Used in Text

A variety of small data files are used in examples throughout this text. Here is a list of where you encounter each.

COINS.SAV

Variables	COIN1
	COIN2

Entered in Chapter 7

GRADES.SAV

Variables:	PRETEST
	MIDTERM
	FINAL
	INSTRUCT
	REQUIRED

Entered in Chapter 6

HEIGHT.SAV

Variables:	HEIGHT
	WEIGHT
	SEX

Entered in Chapter 4

QUESTIONS.SAV

Variables:	Q1
	Q2 (recoded in Chapter 2)
	Q3
	TOTAL (added in Chapter 2)
	GROUP (added in Chapter 2)

Entered in Chapter 2
Modified in Chapter 2

RACE.SAV

Variables: SHORT
                    MEDIUM
                    LONG
                    EXPERIEN

Entered in Chapter 7

SAMPLE.SAV

Variables: ID
                    DAY
                    TIME
                    MORNING
                    GRADE
                    WORK
                    TRAINING (added in Chapter 1)

Entered in Chapter 1
Modified in Chapter 1

SAT.SAV

Variables   SAT
                    GRE
                    GROUP

Entered in Chapter 6

Other Files

For some practice exercises, see Appendix B for needed data sets that are not used in any other examples in the text.